CONJUGAL AMERICA

CONJUGAL AMERICA

On the Public Purposes of Marriage

Allan Carlson

Transaction Publishers
New Brunswick (U.S.A.) and London (U.K.)

First paperback printing 2008
Copyright © 2007 by Transaction Publishers, New Brunswick, New Jersey.

This book is printed on acid-free paper that meets the American National Standard for Permanence of Paper for Printed Library Materials.

Library of Congress Catalog Number: 2006050057
ISBN: 978-0-7658-0362-7 (case); 978-1-4128-0789-0 (paper)
Printed in the United States of America

Library of Congress Cataloging-in-Publication Data

Carlson, Allan C.
    Conjugal America : on the public purposes of marriage / Allan Carlson.
        p. cm.
    Includes bibliographical references and index.
    ISBN 0-7658-0362-3
        1. Marriage—Government policy—United States. 2. Marriages— Religious aspects—Christianity. 3. Human reproduction—Religious aspects— Christianity. 4. Religion and poltics—United States. I. Title.

HQ536.C366   2006
306.850973—dc22   2006050057

For Anders, Sarah-Eva, Anna and Miriam

Contents

Acknowledgements   ix

Introduction   1

1.   Children as the First Purpose of Marriage   5

2.   Two Becoming One Flesh: Marriage as the   23
     Union of the Sexual and the Economic

3.   "Speak Now or Forever Hold Your Peace":   41
     The Communal Nature of Marriage

4.   Standing for Liberty: Marriage, Virtue,   59
     and the Political State

5.   "Conjugal Happiness" and the American Style: 79
     The Special Relationship between Marriage and the
     American Experience

6.   The Necessity of Marriage Policy   97

Appendix   111

Index   133

Acknowledgements

Chapters 1 through 5 of this book began as components of a special lecture series on "The Meaning of Marriage," presented at the Family Research Council in Washington, D.C., during 2004. They appear here with permission. I want to thank those affiliated with the council that year who gave these lectures their encouragement and support, including Allen Crippin II, Colin Stewart, Douglas Minson, Mark Haskew, Peter Sprigg, Bridget Maher, and Tony Perkins. I also need to thank my colleagues at the Howard Center for Family, Religion, and Society in Rockford, Illinois, who provided important help and critical advice, including Heidi Gee, Bryce Christensen, Jean Heise, John Howard, and Larry Jacobs. As always, I am grateful to Transaction's founder and chairman Irving Louis Horowitz, for valued recommendations on reshaping the manuscript, while editor Laurence Mintz did an able job in giving it a fine tuning. My wife of thirty-four years, Elizabeth, provides me a splendid model of helpmate, mother, friend, and advisor. Finally, I dedicate this volume to my children.

Introduction

When "same sex" marriage first emerged as a policy issue in the late 1990s, advocates of the traditional family found themselves in an awkward position. To begin with, they were surprised, even shocked, by this new challenge to an ancient institution, a challenge that seemed to come out of the blue. Only a handful had been following the internal debates in the "gay and lesbian community" during the prior two decades over the best strategies to win public acceptance for their lifestyles. "Conservative gays" saw same-sex marriage as a promising wedge-issue for winning over the American mainstream, an argument opposed by more radical voices who yearned instead for the liberation of homosexuality from all restraints. Well-funded advocacy groups finally settled on the former argument and crafted legal and public relations strategies with patience and skill.

Pro-family advocates also quickly discovered that the cherished institution of marriage was already perilously weak. Changes in the law over the prior three decades, such as the spread of no-fault divorce and broad acquiescence to cultures of divorce and intentional childlessness, had stripped traditional marriage of important legal qualities. For example, the linkage in law and custom of marriage to procreation became vulnerable in an age when a large proportion of marriages occurred between couples unable or unwilling to beget children. As companionship displaced offspring as the guiding reason for marriage, the claims of same-sex couples for recognition gained traction.

Finally, advocates for the traditional family found themselves at a surprising disadvantage in the battle of ideas. While the social sciences were collecting a growing mountain of data confirming the powerful, positive social value of marriage,[1] the public meaning

1

of marriage seemed to be in growing disarray. Cohabitation was in the ascendance. One of every two marriages ended in divorce. Half of married-couple homes were without children. Those homes with children commonly stood empty during the day; mothers and fathers scattered to their separate workplaces with the children in commercial care or at public school. Serial polygamy, rather than fidelity for a lifetime, seemed to be the waxing model. Indeed, marriage appeared as something increasing archaic, an institution no longer suited to an evolving social order. As one contemporary historian concludes:

> ...just as we cannot organize modern political alliances through kinship ties or put the farmers' and skilled craftsmen's households back as the centerpiece of the modern economy, we can never reinstate marriage as the primary source of commitment and care giving in the modern world.[2]

This volume, Conjugal America, seeks to recapture the real purposes and the unchanging nature of this most vital and fundamental human institution. Confronting contemporary issues and drawing heavily on the natural and social sciences, each chapter also reaches into the past to find truths grounded in human experience. This book welcomes the new debate on marriage as an opportunity to revitalize a necessary institution that has recently been abused and neglected.

Chapter 1 reexamines the basic bond of marriage to procreation, showing that this tie has been no less than the foundation of the unwritten sexual constitution of Western civilization. It also shows how the Gnostic heresy, which despises procreation, posed a stark danger to the early Christian movement...and to "the sexual constitution" of our own time as well. Chapter 2 dissects claims regarding the "evolution of marriage," showing that true marriage always represents the vital connection of the sexual with the economic. Marriage renewal, the chapter shows, must rest on the reconstruction of functional, child-rich homes.

Chapter 3 rejects the oft-heard argument that a marriage is simply about the needs and desires of two people. In truth, marriage properly ties the couple to five concentric rings of community:

unborn children, kin, neighborhood, the faith community, and the nation. The political nature of marriage is taken up in chapter 4. It shows why every ambitious totalitarian government seeks above all to destroy marriage, and why the true marital bond actually stands for liberty.

Chapter 5 explores the special place of the institution of marriage in American history, arguing that this nation's past Great Awakenings have been manifested in the renewal of marriage. It suggests that a third Great Awakening may emerge in the early twenty-first century. Chapter 6 argues for the "necessity" of marriage policy. Both the nature of the centralizing state and the pressures of modernity have altered family circumstances. New protections and encouragements to marriage are now imperative. The book concludes with specific recommendations.

Notes

1. Early summaries included: Glenn T. Stanton, *Why Marriage Matters: Reasons to Believe in Marriage in Postmodern Society* (Colorado Springs, CO: Pinon Press, 1997; Linda J. White and Maggie Gallagher, *The Case for Marriage: Why Married People are Happier, Healthier, and Better off Financially* (New York: Doubleday, 2002); and Bridget Maher, *The Family Portrait: A Compilation of Data, Research and Public Opinion on the Family* (Washington, DC: Family Research Council, 2002).

2. Stephanie Coontz, *Marriage: A History* (New York: Viking, 2005): 313.

1

Children as the First Purpose of Marriage

When Massachusetts officials, facing the court case *Goodridge v. Department of Public Health*, set out to defend that state's marriage law from a challenge by seven homosexual couples, their major line of defense was procreation. Making babies, the state argued, was the first purpose of marriage. By definition, same-sex partners could not create a child as a couple. This was important, the argument continued, because children usually do best when growing up with their two natural parents. Moreover, requiring fertility tests before marriage by opposite sex couples would be cumbersome and overly intrusive. It was better to let all otherwise qualified opposite sex couples to marry than to go down that troubling regulatory path.

And the initial trial court, let us remember, agreed with the state. The judge ruled that the primary purpose of marriage, under Massachusetts law, was, in fact, procreation. Accordingly, the court concluded that the state could reasonably distinguish between homosexual claimants to marriage and those heterosexual couples that were at least "theoretically...capable" of procreation without relying on "inherently more cumbersome" non-coital reproductive methods.[1]

Even Evan Wolfson, the acknowledged leader of the "gay marriage" movement, has agreed that

> At first glance, the "basic biology" argument seems to make some sense. After all, it doesn't take more than a fourth-grade health class education to know that men's and women's bodies in some sense "complement each other" and that when a man and a woman come "together as one flesh" it often leads to procreation. [2]

5

But of course, the trial court decision did not survive appeal to the Massachusetts Supreme Judicial Court. This higher court, on a 4-3 vote, dismissed the procreation argument, pointing to opposite sex couples in which the woman was over childbearing age or that were otherwise infertile. Could the state "rationally" tell them that they could not marry? It could not. Indeed, the Court noted that, under state law, even those "who cannot stir from their death bed may marry," provided they were of the opposite sex. Moreover, infertility was not a ground for divorce, and by inference so not a bar to marriage either. In addition, the Court noted that Massachusetts law protected the parental rights of homosexuals and allowed same-sex couples to adopt children. It was irrational for the state so to enable "gay parenting" while also denying the children involved the benefits of "family stability and economic security" found in a marital home.

Evan Wolfson also moves on to dissect the procreation argument, finding it actually "riddled with holes." If procreation is the purpose of marriage, he argues, then the marriages of Bob and Elizabeth Dole, John and Teresa Heinz Kerry, and Pat and Shelley Buchanan should all be declared invalid. So should the marriage of the Father of our County, George Washington, to Martha, which produced no children. Another same-sex activist, Dale Carpenter, argues that if there was any merit to the procreation argument,

> We would require prospective married couples to sign an affidavit stating that they are able to procreate and intend to procreate. If in, say, 10 years they had not procreated, we could presume they are unable or unwilling to do so and could dissolve the marriage as unworthy of the unique institution.

He adds that since no one has really proposed this, or anything like it, it is clear that the defenders of marriage "do not take the narrow procreationist view of marriage very seriously." Instead, he says, the traditionalists impose another rule: "Nobody is required to procreate in order to marry, except gay couples." Such discrimination, he implies, could not survive a test by the "equal protection clause" of the Fourteenth Amendment.[3] Indeed, that usually faithful conservative Supreme Court Justice, Antonin Scalia, in his 2003 dissent in *Lawrence* v. *Texas*, noted:

If moral disapprobation of homosexual conduct is "no state interest" for purposes of proscribing [private adult sex], what justification could there possibly be for denying the benefits of marriage to homosexual couples? Surely not the encouragement of procreation, since the sterile and the elderly are allowed to marry.[4]

It is fair to conclude, I think, that the procreation argument is in serious trouble.

My purpose here is to examine the bond between marriage and procreation. Where did this linkage come from? Why is it no longer self-evident? What earlier developments weakened the procreative nature of marriage? And: Is it possible to salvage this appeal to procreation in the same-sex marriage debate?

Sex and Civilization

Turning to the first question—where did the bond between marriage and procreation come from?—my answer is simple: It is no less than the foundation for what we might call the unwritten sexual constitution of our civilization.

Nearly two thousand years ago, what would become Western Christian civilization began to take form in a time of great sexual disorder. The moral and family disciplines of the old Roman Republic were gone, replaced by the intoxications of empire. Slave concubinage flourished in these years. Divorce by mutual consent was easy, and common. Adultery was chic, and widespread. Homosexuality was a frequent practice, particularly in man-boy sexual relations. There was a callous disregard for infant life, with infanticide a regular practice. Caesar Augustus, worried about the plummeting Roman birthrate, even implemented the so-called "Augustan Laws" in 18 BC, measures that punished adultery, penalized childlessness, and showered benefits on families with three or more children. These laws may have slowed, but did not reverse, the moral and social deterioration.

Between 50 and 300 AD, and out of this same chaos, the Fathers of the Christian Church crafted a new sexual order. Procreative marriage served as its foundation. Importantly, they also built this new order in reaction to the Gnostic heresies which threatened the young church; indeed, which threatened all human life.

The Gnostic idea rose independent of Christianity, but I am concerned here with so-called Christian Gnosticism. The Gnostics drew together myths from Persia, Jewish magic and mysticism, Greek philosophy, and Chaldean mystical speculation. More troubling, they also appealed to the freedom from the law as proclaimed by Christ and Paul. In this sense, they were antinomians; that is, they believed that the Gospel freed Christians from obedience to any law, be it scriptural, civil, or moral. The Gnostics claimed to have a special "gnosis," a unique wisdom, a "secret knowledge" denied to ordinary Christians. They appealed to unseen spirits. They denied nature. They developed a mélange of moral and doctrinal ideas. But virtually all Gnostics did share two views: they rejected marriage as a child-related institution; and they scorned procreation.

This heresy posed a grave challenge to the early Christian movement. Indeed, the Epistles are replete with warnings against Gnostic teachings. In 1 *Timothy* 4, for example, Paul writes that "some will depart from the faith by giving heed to deceitful spirits and doctrines of demons….who forbid marriage." In *Jude* 4 we read that admission into the Christian community "has been secretly gained by…ungodly persons who pervert the grace of our God into licentiousness." 2 *Peter* tells of false prophets corrupting the young church, "irrational animals, creatures of instinct…. reveling in their dissipation, carousing with you. They have eyes full of adultery, insatiable souls." Similar warnings or admonitions are found in 1 *Corinthians* (5:1-8; 6:12-13), *Romans* (6:1; 8:2), Philippians (3:18), Galatians (5:13), 2 *Timothy* (3:6-7), *Ephesians* (5:5-7), and *Revelation* (2:14-15). Simon Magus, described in *Acts*, chapter 8, was most probably a Gnostic, evidenced by his use of magic.

Relative to sex, Gnosticism took two forms. One strand emphasized total sexual license, endless sexual experimentation. Claiming the freedom of the Gospel, these Gnostics indulged in adultery, homosexuality, and ritualistic fornication. The Church Father Clement described abuse of the Eucharist by the Gnostics in the church of Alexandria:

> There are some who call Aphrodite Pandemos [physical love] a mystical communion….[T]hey have impiously called by the name of communion any common sexual intercourse….These thrice-wretched

men treat carnal and sexual intercourse as a sacred religious mystery, and think that it will bring them to the Kingdom of God.[5]

Other Gnostics of this sort taught that "marrying and bearing [children] are from Satan"; that sexual intercourse by "spiritual men," in and of itself, would hasten the coming of the Pleroma, or the fullness of the divine hierarchy of the eons; and that the true believer should have every possible sexual experience.

In marked contrast to this polymorphous perversity, the other Gnostic strand totally rejected sexuality. Tatian, for example, led a faction called the Encratites, or "the self-controlled." They saw marriage as corruption and fornication, and demanded lifelong abstinence. In the non-canonical *Gospel According to the Egyptians*, Salome asks: "How long shall men die?" Jesus is said to answer: "As long as you women bear children." From this, these Gnostics concluded that they could defeat death by ceasing procreation. They also celebrated androgyny, since a being without sexual identity could obviously not be procreative. The non-canonical *Gospel of Thomas* has Jesus saying: "Every woman who makes herself male enters the Kingdom of Heaven." The evil of the world denied the bearing of children; the celibate alone would enjoy the Kingdom of God.

Considering these two Gnostic forms, historian John Noonan summarizes:

> The whole thrust of the antinomian [Gnostic] current was to devalue marriage, to deprive marital relations of any particular purpose, and to value sexual intercourse as experience [alone].[6]

Within the broad context of a Roman civilization sliding into family breakdown and sexual hedonism, the young Christian church faced as well this infiltration of life-denying, socially destructive ideas into its own ranks. For Christian leaders, the great question became: Just what is marriage for?

Christian Marriage

Answers came from several sources. The Church Fathers noted, for example, the fierce hatred shown by the Gnostics for the Hebrew Scriptures. From Judaism, accordingly, the Church Fathers could see children as a Divine blessing for their parents and for the community as a whole. As told in *Deuteronomy*:

> And because you hearken to these ordinances, and keep and do them, the Lord your God will keep with you the covenant and the steadfast love which he swore to your fathers to keep; he will love you, bless you, and multiply you; he will also bless the fruit of your body....You shall be blessed above all peoples; there shall not be male or female barren among you....[7]

Genesis was also filled with promises from God to the patriarchs that their wives should be fruitful and that the Lord "will multiply your descendants as the stars of heaven and as the sand which is upon the seashore."[8] Throughout the centuries, the Jewish sages had declared that "One without children is considered as though dead." Another early source stated that "he who does not engage in procreation is as if he diminished the Divine image."[9]

Another Jewish inspiration may have been the small, ascetic Essene community, now famed for compiling the Dead Sea Scrolls. According to the first-century AD historian Josephus, members of this order entered marriages "not for self-indulgence, but for the procreation of children."[10]

Still another source may have been Philo, a Jew trained in Greek philosophy, who expressed revulsion over pagan Roman pleasure-seeking. "Like a bad husbandman," he wrote, "[the homosexual] spends his labor night and day on soil from which no growth at all can be expected." The sexual act was for procreation, Philo insisted. Seeking a consistent sexual standard, he even reached a novel conclusion, condemning marriage to women known to be sterile.[11]

Another source for early Christian leaders was the Stoic ideal. Also filled with revulsion over the sexual excesses of first-century Rome, the Stoics—including philosophers such as Epictetus and Musonius Rufus—summoned reason to control human desires and behavior. Moderation in all things, including sexuality, was their goal. They also held that there was a natural law which gave purpose to human life and which revealed acts unworthy of human beings. Sexual intercourse in marriage, the Stoics concluded, found its clear and natural purpose in the propagation of the human race.

However, intercourse only for pleasure was suspect. As the first-century Stoic, Seneca, declared,

> All love of another's wife is shameful; so too, too much love of your own. A wise man ought to love his wife with judgment, not affection. Let him control his impulses and not be borne headlong into copulation. Nothing is fouler than to love a wife like an adulteress.... Let them show themselves to their wives not as lovers, but as husbands.[12]

Or as another Stoic text explained,

> ...we have intercourse not for pleasure, but for the maintenance of the species.[13]

It is clear that these Stoic teachings had a particularly strong effect on the Church Father, Clement of Alexandria. Indeed, according to John Noonan, Clement's influential work on the purposes of Christian marriage was simply "a paraphrase" of the Stoic, Musonius Rufus.[14]

And of course, these early Christian leaders also drew on the Gospels and the letters of Paul. The orthodox Gospel texts showed Jesus attending the wedding feast at Cana and performing there his first miracle, turning water into wine. Jesus also condemned adultery and divorce. In 1 *Timothy* 2:15, Paul taught that "woman will be saved through bearing children." And in *Ephesians* 5, he equated the marital love of husband and wife to the bond between Christ and his Church:

> Wives, be subject to your husbands, as to the Lord. For the husband is the head of the wife as Christ is the head of the Church.... Husbands, love your wives, as Christ loved the Church and gave himself up for her.... "For this reason a man shall leave his father and mother and be joined to his wife, and the two shall become one." This is a great mystery....[15]

All of these sources led the early Church Fathers to one conclusion: the purpose of marriage is procreation. While also celebrating lifelong chastity, they refused to abandon the need for children. As Justin explained in the mid-second century: "We Christians either marry only to produce children, or, if we refuse to marry, are completely continent." Two centuries later, John Chrysostom taught that "there are two reasons why marriage was instituted, that we may live chastely and that we may become parents." In the year 400, Augustine, the bishop of Hippo, wrote the book, *The Good of Marriage*. He argued that God desired man's perpetuation through marriage. Offspring, he insisted, were the obvious and first "good" of marriage (the other two being fidelity and symbolic stability or sacrament). As Augustine explained,

> What food is to the health of man, intercourse is to the health of the human race, and each is not without its carnal delight which cannot be lust if, modified and restrained by temperance, it is brought to a natural use [i.e., procreation].

Augustine also insisted that the act of procreation included "the receiving of [children] lovingly, the nourishing of them humanely, the educating of them religiously."[16]

A Lasting Morality

In this way, the bond of marriage to procreation became the social and moral foundation for emerging Western Christian civilization. The sexual disorders of the late Roman Empire and the anti-human fanaticism of the Gnostics faced defeat by a new marital morality. And, as articulated by Augustine in the year 400 AD, this moral order lasted for another 1,500 years. Even the tremors of the Protestant Reformation in the sixteenth century probably did more to strengthen, than weaken, this powerful tie between procreation and marriage. Martin Luther, for example, believed that God's words in *Genesis* 1:28, "Be fruitful and multiply," represented more than a command; they were, he said, "a divine ordinance which it is not our prerogative to hinder or ignore."[17] This led him to reject celibacy as a special spiritual state and to encourage even priests, monks, and nuns to marry and have children. As Luther wrote,

> We were all created to do as our parents have done, to beget and rear children. This is a duty which God has lain upon us, commanded, and implanted in us, as is proved by our bodily members, our daily emotions, and the example of all mankind.[18]

It is true that Protestantism did inject more passion and intimacy into the marital bond than was considered seemly by the early

Church Fathers. Still, these emotions remained tightly bound to procreation. Consider, for example, this poem written by the Puritan wife, Anne Bradstreet, to her husband Simon, who—ironically—was among the founders of the Massachusetts Bay Colony in 1630. It is entitled "A Letter to Her Husband, Absent upon Publick Employment":

> I like the earth this season, mourn in black,
> My Sun is gone so far in's Zodiack,
> Whom whilst I 'joy'd, nor storms, nor frosts I felt,
> His warmth such frigid colds did cause to melt.
> My chilled limbs now nummed lye forlorn;
> Return, return sweet Sol from Capricorn;
> In this dead time, alas, what can I more
> Than view those fruits which through thy heat I bore.[19]

The "fruits" referred to here are, of course, their children, the offspring of Christian marital ardor and love.

Closer to our time, attitudes toward birth control revealed the continuing strength of the bond between marriage and procreation. Even in the late nineteenth century, the free-love feminists then emerging in New England refused to endorse birth control. According to the feminist historian Linda Gordon,

> The basis for this reluctance lies in their awareness that a consequence of effective contraception would be the separation of sexuality from reproduction. A state of things that permitted sexual intercourse to take place normally, even frequently, without the risk of pregnancy inevitably seemed to nineteenth-century middle class women to be an attack on the family.[20]

As late as 1917, the unwritten sexual constitution of our civilization—crafted nearly two thousand years before—remained intact. No less a body than the Massachusetts Supreme Judicial Court ruled that year in favor of a law prohibiting the distribution of contraceptives. As the Massachusetts Court reasoned:

> [The law's] plain purpose is to protect purity, to preserve chastity, to encourage continence and self restraint, to defend the sanctity of the home, and thus to engender in the State and nation a virile and virtuous race of men and women.[21]

On Contraception

However, this appeal to "a virile and virtuous race of men and women," and implicitly to the tight bond between marriage and procreation, would unravel over the balance of the twentieth century. This story could be told many ways; I want to focus simply on two episodes: specifically, the legalization of contraception in America; and the disappearance of the concept of illegitimacy in Sweden.

Regarding the first, Evan Wolfson writes in his new book *Why Marriage Matters*:

> To hear the opponents of gay equality today, one would not know that for decades the law of the land…has been to recognize that marriage is not just about procreation—indeed it is not necessarily about procreation at all.[22]

In this statement, he is unfortunately correct. The U.S. Supreme Court's 1965 ruling in *Griswold* v. *Connecticut* stands in ever sharper relief as a profound break in American, and Western history. At issue was a Connecticut law prohibiting the use of contraceptives. Authored by Justice William O. Douglas, the Court's opinion overturned this measure. In doing so, the Court also claimed to discover, for the first time, "penumbras" around and "emanations" from the Bill of Rights, new legal spirits which created "zones of privacy" hitherto unknown. (Curiously, such strange language would have been familiar to a first-century Gnostic.) Almost cynically, given what came later, the Court appealed to "the sacred precincts of marital bedrooms" and to "the notions of privacy surrounding the marriage relationship" to justify its decision. Indeed, the opinion concluded,

> We deal with a right of privacy older than the Bill of Rights—older than our political parties, older than our school system. Marriage is a coming together for better or for worse, hopefully enduring and intimate to the degree of being sacred…. [I]t is an association for as noble a purpose as any involved in our prior decisions.[23]

In truth, *Griswold* represented a direct assault on our civilization's unwritten sexual constitution. As Wolfson correctly states, "The Court recognized [in *Griswold*] the right not to procreate in marriage." Indeed, only six years later, in the case *Eisenstadt* v. *Baird*, the Supreme Court appealed to the same "penumbras" and "emanations" from the Bill of Rights, to the same "right of privacy," in order to declare marriage largely empty of meaning:

> It is true that in *Griswold* the right of privacy in question inhered in the marital relationship. Yet the marital couple is not an independent entity with a mind and heart of its own, but an association of two individuals each with a separate intellectual and emotional makeup. If the right of privacy means anything, it is the right of the individual, married or single, to be free from unwarranted governmental intrusion into matters so fundamentally affecting a person as the decision whether to bear or beget a child.[24]

With this decision, the "penumbras" and "emanations" of the Constitution denied the substance of both marriage and the natural law. A year later, 1973, the same new wisdom led the Supreme Court to overturn the abortion laws of all fifty states, creating a new "right to abortion" (again, a right that would surely have pleased the baby-hating Gnostics). In 1992, the Court appealed to "the right to define one's own concept of existence, of meaning, of the universe, and of the mystery of human life" in its reaffirmation of abortion rights.[25] (This language is very close to a definition of the Gnostic idea). And in 2003, the Court in *Lawrence* v. *Texas* summoned the same "penumbras" and "emanations" to find a right to uninhibited sexual expression, a right to sodomy (yet again, the Gnostics would have understood and been pleased).

On Illegitimacy

The decline and fall of the concept of "illegitimacy" also points to the disappearance of the bond between marriage and procreation. The cultural and legal term, "illegitimate birth," obviously sought to use fear and shame to help confine sexual relations and childbearing to marriage. It was also part and parcel of our civilization's unwritten sexual constitution. And yet, most of us are bothered by the term today. To the contemporary way of thinking, it punishes innocent children for the mistakes of their parents. Even so, the concept proved highly resilient...until the end of the twentieth century.

There were earlier attempts to banish the term. During the French Revolution, the Law of 12 Brumaire (November 2, 1793) intended to sweep away all laws that distinguished between legitimate and illegitimate children. "There are no bastards in France!" the revolutionaries triumphantly declared in 1794. And yet the change was opposed in the countryside, and never really enforced by the Courts. The law was repealed in 1803.

In 1918, the Bolshevik revolutionaries in Russia also abolished "illegitimacy," with the new Soviet Family Law Code stating:

> Birth itself shall be the basis of the family. No differentiation whatsoever shall be made between relationship by birth in or out of wedlock.

This was part of the larger Communist project to eliminate marriage and the natural family altogether. As Nikolai Bukharin told the 1924 Congress of the Communist Party of the Soviet Union: "The family is a formidable stronghold of all the turpitudes of the old regime." It had to go. Divorce on request by either spouse and the equation of cohabitation with marriage were other parts of the Communist project. The law also imposed a duty of support on unmarried fathers. And yet, these reforms did not work. Child abandonment grew common. Vagrant children filled the land. In the end, even Joseph Stalin acknowledged failure. A new Family Code, introduced in 1944, specified that only a registered marriage created rights and duties between husband and wife, parent and child. The idea of "illegitimacy" returned.[26]

However, a far more successful project to abolish "illegitimacy" occurred in Sweden during the last three decades of the twentieth century. It succeeded only by simultaneously deconstructing marriage and substituting a massive welfare state for the home.

Back in 1915, Sweden had already removed the terms "legitimate" and "illegitimate" from its legal codes, inserting "born in/out of wedlock" instead. While of moral, symbolic, and long-term importance, the change had no immediate impact. Into the early 1960s, Swedish family life remained relatively strong and vital. It was only during Sweden's so-called "Red Years," 1967-76, that real changes occurred. Under heavy feminist influence, the Democratic

Socialist government set out to abolish the roles of husband and wife, to make divorce easy, to eliminate marriage as an economic unit, and to raise the status of cohabitation to equality with marriage. Notably, in 1976—at the very end of this radical reform—the government deleted the terms "born in/out of wedlock" from all its statutes. This fully severed the legal bond between marriage and procreation. To make this work, the Social Democrats also had to expand the welfare state, with government now supplying most of the support and care of children once given by families, from universal health insurance to massive day care subsidies to state child allowances to school meals. With the home so dismantled, and with procreation already unrelated to marriage, it was an easy and logical step to extend marriage-like "registered partnerships" to same-sex couples in 1995.[27]

The leveling "right of privacy" in America; the triumph of socialism over the home in Sweden: both contributed to the successful repeal of the sexual constitution of Western civilization, which had rested on the fundamental bond of marriage to procreation.

The New Gnostics

So where are we left? It is important to realize that the contemporary foe of marriage is something at once new and different, and as old as time. The Gnostic idea is back, in new guise. It shapes everything from modern feminist theology (consider Elaine Pagel's bestselling *Beyond Belief: The Secret Gospel of Thomas*),[28] to popular literature (The *Da Vinci Code*, 200 weeks on the New York Times best-seller list, is an openly Gnostic text), even to—as I have implied—the reasoning of our highest court. Nothing that is natural, traditional, cultural, religious, social, or moral is safe from the Gnostic idea. And no appeal to nature, to history, to civilization, or to human experience of any kind can prevail against the "special knowledge" of the modern antinomians who dominate the contemporary culture.

Can one still defend the purpose of marriage as procreation? No, not in the current Constitutional climate. It is now clear that the "right of privacy," conceived by the Supreme Court nearly four decades ago, is the enemy of both marriage and procreation separately, and is especially hostile when they are united. It is also clear that key battles in defense of this union were lost decades ago, long before anyone even imagined same-sex marriage. And these battles were over questions that relatively few contemporary Americans are really prepared to reopen. How many are ready to urge the recriminalization of contraception? How many want to argue for a strict legal and cultural imposition of the word, "illegitimate," on certain little children? One might imagine a new effort to repeal the "equal protection" clause of the Fourteenth Amendment tied to language that denied the existence of "the right of privacy." But even before facing the enormous political issues so raised, it would be unlikely to work. The Supreme Court has made clear that the subversive "right of privacy" is older and more fundamental than the Constitution itself, and that it "emanates" from the "penumbra" of the Bill of Rights. Mere words—even of a new Amendment—are unlikely to contain these "penumbras" and "emanations."

Instead, the defenders of marriage are left for now with strictly political options: the raw exercise of influence. Both those bills that would strip the federal courts of jurisdiction over marriage and the proposed Federal Marriage Amendment could build firewalls around the already battered institution of marriage, protecting it from further depredations by the "right of privacy." Of course, there is no guarantee that a future Supreme Court might not rule that the "right of privacy" and the "equal protection" clause trump these innovations as well, so bringing on a Constitutional crisis. All the same, such efforts are worth pursuing.

Outside the Box

Are there other political acts that would reconnect procreation and marriage? Perhaps, if advocates are prepared to think "outside the box." For example, they could turn their opponents' key arguments back on them. They could restrict some of the legal and welfare benefits of civil marriage solely to those married during their time of natural, procreative potential: for women, below the age of forty-five or so (for men, in the Age of Viagra, the line would admittedly be harder to draw). The idea is not without recent political precedence. Back in 1969, Representative Wilbur Mills—the then powerful chairman of the House Ways and Means Committee—wanted to respond to complaints by unmarried adults that existing tax law unfairly favored the married. It was true that the existing practice of "income splitting" by married couples on their joint tax returns, in the context of high marginal tax rates, did give a strong tax benefit to marriage. Importantly, though, Mills stated that he wanted to preserve this "marriage bonus" for the young and fertile, while still helping those whom he labeled (in now archaic language) as "spinsters." Accordingly, he proposed maintaining the benefits of income splitting only for married persons under the age of thirty-five. (This approach, I do note in passing, went nowhere. The Nixon administration and Congress chose instead to reduce the benefits of income splitting for all married persons; and they so unwittingly created the "marriage penalty" with which policymakers still grapple today).

Another, and perhaps more realistic way to rebind marriage and procreation would be, counterintuitively, to take some of the benefits currently attached to marriage and reroute them instead through children. Allow me one practical example here. Whatever the future, it is likely that most households with two or more children will continue to be married-couple, natural-parent homes. These are still, and always will be, the places most open to "a full quiver." Advocates could encourage them by tying retirement benefits to family size: that is, the more children that a couple brought into the world, the higher their later monthly Social Security benefit. Or, marriage advocates could create a new tax credit against payroll taxes: rebating, say, 20 percent of the current 15.3 percent tax facing parents for each child born. Again, these ideas would indirectly favor child-rich homes; and most of these, in the American context, would predictably contain a married couple.

These approaches are, admittedly, tangential. However, bolder steps are all but impossible until there are profound changes in the membership and thinking of our highest court; and until we the people actually want to restore the unwritten sexual constitution of our civilization, including the hard parts. It may be that the first requirement—changing the court—will prove easier to achieve than the second.

Notes

1. Quotations from: Johanna Grossman, "Are Bans on Same-Sex Marriage Constitutional?" at: *http://writ.news.findlaw.com/grossman/2003.1120. html* (10/4/2004).
2. Evan Wolfson, *Why Marriage Matters: America, Equality, and Gay People's Right to Marry* (New York: Simon & Schuster, 2004): 75.
3. Dale Carpenter, "Gay Marriage and Procreation," *Bay Area Reporter* (March 18, 2004).
4. Lawrence v. Texas (02-102) 41 S.W. 3rd 349 (2003).
5. In John T. Noonan, *Contraception: A History of Its Treatment by the Catholic Theologians and Canonists* (Cambridge, MA: Harvard University Press, 1986): 64.
6. Noonan, *Contraception*, p. 8.
7. *Deuteronomy* 7: 12-14; all Biblical texts cited are from The Revised Standard Version of 1952.
8. Genesis 22:17.
9. *Babylonian Talmum Nedarim* 64b and 63b. Cited in Lewis D. Solomon, *The Jewish Tradition, Sexuality and Procreation* (Lanham, MD: University Press of America, 2002): 89-91.
10. Josephus, *The Jewish War*, edited and translated by H. St. John Thackery (Cambridge, MA: Harvard University Press, 1961): 2.120, 160.
11. Philo, *The Special Laws* 3.36; quoted in Noonan, *Contraception*, p. 54.
12. Seneca, *Fragments*, ed. Friedrich G. Haase (Leipzig: Teubner, 1897); no. 84.
13. *The Nature of the Universe*, section 44; in Richard Harder, editor, *Ocellus Lucanus* (Berlin: Weidman, 1926).
14. Noonan, *Contraception*, p. 48.
15. *Ephesians* 5:22-23, 25, 31-32.
16. Augustine, *On Genesis According to the Letter* 9.7, CSEL 28: 276; in Noonan, Contraception, p. 56.
17. Martin Luther, *The Estate of Marriage* [1520], in *Luther's Works*. Vol.45: *The Christian in Society* (Philadelphia: Muhlenburg Press, 1962): 18.
18. Martin Luther, *An Exhortation to the Knights of the Teutonic Order That They Lay Aside False Chastity and Assume the True Chastity of Wedlock* [1523], in Luther's Works, Vol. 45, p. 155.
19. Found in: Harrison T. Meserole, *Seventeenth-Century American Poetry* (New York: New York University Press, 1968): 32-33.
20. Linda Gordon, *Woman's Body, Woman's Right* (London and New York: Penguin Books, 1974 [1999]): 107.
21. *Commonwealth* v. *Allison*, 227 Mass. 57, 62, 116 N. E. 266 (1917).

22. Wolfson, *Why Marriage Matters*, p. 79.

23. *Griswold* v. *Connecticut*, 381 U.S. 479 (1965).

24. *Eisenstadt* v. *Baird*, 405 U.S. 438 (1972).

25. *Planned Parenthood of Southeastern Pa.* v. *Casey,* 505 U.S. 833 (1992).

26. Jenny Teichman, *Illegitimacy: An Examination of Bastardy* (Ithaca, NY: Cornell University Press, 1982): 153-61.

27. Teichman, *Illegitimacy*, pp. 168-71; and D. Bradley, "Marriage, Family, Property and Inheritance in Swedish Law," *International and Comparative Law Quarterly* 39 (April 1990): 373-84.

28. Elaine Pagels, *Beyond Belief: The Secret Gospel of Thomas* (Westminster, MD: Random House, 2003); also Rosemary Radford Ruether, *Christianity and the Making of the Modern Family* (Boston: Beacon, Press, 2000).

2

Two Becoming One Flesh: Marriage as the Union of the Sexual and the Economic

"As time marches inexorably on, human society...evolves." So philosophized Judge William L. Downing in striking down the state of Washington's Defense of Marriage Act in August, 2004, ruling that same-sex couples have a right to marry.

Indeed, evolutionary language seems tightly bound to the "gay marriage" agenda. "There is an evolution of society," cooed Canadian prime minister Jean Chretien in 2003 when announcing a new national policy opening marriage to homosexual couples.[1] Jacqueline Murray, columnist for the *Toronto Globe and Mail*, agrees that evolution is at work here: "Extending marriage to people of the same sex may be the final frontier and the logical conclusion of this evolution."[2] Writing in the *Boston Globe*, Virginia Postrel argues that social institutions such as marriage are themselves "the result of an evolutionary process"; gay marriage, as such, represents another promising "experiment in living" contributing to forward evolution.[3] Columnist Ellen Goodman concludes that the Massachusetts Supreme Judicial Court's ruling that homosexuals have a right to marriage "may be as evolutionary as it is historic," adding: "The evolution of gay rights and marriage laws now merge into the definition of marriage written by the Massachusetts court."[4]

This focus on evolution is revealing and important. It points toward the ideology that drives the same-sex marriage campaign, and the deeper conflict of ideas in which we are now engaged.

On the one hand, there is the view put forth by prominent early anthropologists that marriage is, in essence, an unchanging institution, universal to humanity. As Edward Westermarck explained over 100 years ago: "Among the lowest savages, as well as the most civilized races of men, we find the family consisting of parents and children, and the father as its protector." Holding this family system together was marriage, combining "a regulated sexual relation" with "economic obligations." In Westermarck's view, distinct maternal, paternal, and marital instincts all existed, each rooted in human nature. Indeed, he said that "the institution of marriage…has developed out of a primeval habit." While variations in the details could be found in different human cultures, the fundamental marriage bond was unchanging.[5] Or as George Murdock wrote in his great 1949 anthropological survey: "The nuclear family is a universal human social grouping." Moreover, "[a]ll known human societies have developed specialization and cooperation between the sexes roughly along this biologically determined line of cleavage." Murdock concluded,

> …marriage exists only when the economic and the sexual are united into one relationship, and this combination only occurs in marriage. Marriage, thus defined, is found in every known human society.[6]

The conservative defense of marriage implicitly appeals to this vision of a necessary and unchanging institution, rooted in human nature.

"The Evolution of Marriage"

On the other hand, a different theory of marriage has exerted a profound influence, from the 1880s to our day. As one prominent sociologist has explained, "Social science developed only one comprehensive theory of family change, one based on nineteenth century evolutionary ideas."[7] Applying Charles Darwin's concept of "natural selection" to human behavior, these theorists have argued that human marriage is an evolving institution. As we have already seen, this very notion—and the theory behind it—today drives one major argument for same-sex marriage. Where did this theory come from? What does this theory of social evolution say? How has it affected American views in the past? Does it bear any truth?

The classic formulation of "the evolution of marriage" idea is found in Lewis Morgan's 1877 book, *Ancient Society*. In fact, this book was the result of a U.S. government investigation of the social lives of the American Indians. Morgan focused particular attention on the Iroquois, but drew broader conclusions. In his view, the family was an active agent, never stationary, moving in evolutionary fashion from lower to higher forms. The three main stages in this process, he said, were:

- Among pre-historic savages, group marriage, where unrestricted sexual intercourse existed within a tribe, such that every woman belonged to every man, and every man to every woman. Sexual orgies were routine practices. In this perfectly promiscuous social order, Morgan argued, children were common to all and descent or lineage was traced through the mother's family, the maternal "gens," since paternity could not be established. This, in turn, gave power and authority to women.
- Among barbarians, the pairing family. This construct rested on the nuclear pairing off of one man to one woman, and a limitation on inbreeding through creation of the incest taboo. And yet, the pairing family still held on to remnants of the old ways, as where sisters would be the mutual wives of their mutual husbands, and where maternal lineage would remain primary. Still, enforcement of the incest taboo led to an evolutionary advance, Morgan said, including the expansion of human skulls and brains.
- Finally, among civilized people, the monogamous family, resting on patriarchal controls and enforced chastity and fidelity among women, in order to ensure the fathers' lineage.[8]

Other ethnographers quickly exposed the flaws in Morgan's analysis. However, his theory soon took on an ideological life of its own. The writer drawing out the political implications of Morgan's work was Friedrich Engels, co-author of *The Communist Manifesto*. In his 1884 book, *The Origin of the Family, Private Property, and the State*, Engels underscored Morgan's importance:

The discovery [of] the original maternal "gens" has the same signification for primeval history that Darwin's theory of evolution had for biology and Marx's theory of surplus value for political economy.

From a communist, high praise indeed! And yet, in an important break with Morgan, Engels refused to see the modern monogamous marriage as superior or good. Indeed:

> Monogamy…does by no means enter history as a reconciliation of man and wife and still less as the highest form of marriage. On the contrary, it enters as the subjugation of one sex by the other, as the proclamation of an antagonism between the sexes unknown in all preceding history.

Specifically, Engels denied that romantic sexual love could survive in monogamous marriage. Moreover, he said that the human urge for primeval group marriage survived even in civilized nations through a turn to prostitutes by the men, and to adultery by the women.

Engels also laid out how the pending communist revolution will allow an evolutionary return to group marriage. Action components included:

1. Put all women into outside labor: "…the emancipation of women is primarily dependent on the reintroduction of the whole female sex into the public industries."
2. Socialize property: "With the transformation of the means of production into collective property the monogamous family ceases to be the economic unit of society. The private household changes to a social industry. The care and education of children becomes a social matter."
3. Free love: "Will not this be sufficient cause for…a more un-conventional intercourse of the sexes and a more lenient public opinion regarding virgin honor and female shame?"
4. And "No Fault" Divorce: "If marriage founded on love is alone moral, then it follows that marriage is moral only as long as love lasts."[9]

Where the essentialist, conservative view of marriage saw changes as either a weakening or strengthening of the normative institution, Engels' evolutionist view held to a teleological end involving a post-marriage, post-family social order.

Losing the Economic Function

I dwell on Engels here because a watered-down version of this Marxist evolutionary understanding spread far and deep in the

United States, working to undermine both the economic and the sexual aspects of marriage. To this day, no matter how carefully camouflaged, the Cultural Left's arguments for societal "evolution" (including the "evolution" toward same-sex marriage) still commonly derive from Engel's profound misinterpretation of Morgan's discredited work.

Regarding the economic function, for example, the first important *Social History of the American Family* appeared in 1917, complete with the familiar evolutionary argument. "American history consummates the disappearance of the wider familism and the substitution of the parentalism of society," wrote historian Arthur Calhoun. Since natural parents were, by and large, unfit for parenthood in the new order, society came "to accept as a duty" the upbringing of the young. Ever more children passed "into the custody of community experts who are qualified to perform the complexer functions of parenthood…which the parents have neither the time nor knowledge to perform." Calhoun concluded,

> The new view is that the higher and more obligatory relation is to society rather than to the family; the family goes back to the age of savagery while the state belongs to the age of civilization. The modern individual is a world citizen, served by the world and home interests can no longer be supreme.[10]

Another influential, sanitized version of marriage and family structures in evolution appeared in the work of sociologist William Ogburn, of the University of Chicago. An analytical Marxist, Ogburn emphasized that the prime force in history was technology, or "material culture," and that after a period of time, what he called "culture lag," social institutions would adjust to the new material realities. Commissioned by President Herbert Hoover's Research Committee on Social Trends to examine family life, Ogburn described in 1933 an American marriage and family system steadily diminishing. Once "the chief economic institution, the factory of the time, producing almost all that men needed," the family now stood stripped of all productive tasks, these having passed to the factories. At the same time, "the educational and protective functions" of the family had gone to government, because state institutions had "greater technical efficiency." Already by the 1930s, he reported, American homes "are merely 'parking places' for parents and children who spend their active hours elsewhere." Even so, "the evidence points to the further transfer of functions from the home," including the care of pre-school children.[11]

During the 1940s and 1950s, prominent sociologists called "functionalists" attempted to take this bad news about the evolutionary loss of family functions and turn it into a positive good. Talcott Parsons of Harvard University, the leader of this school of thought, acknowledged that among Americans "many of the 'auxiliary' functions [of the family], such as those of economic production which are common in kinship units, are here reduced to a minimum." But this was all to the good, he said, for it made modern families sleek and efficient, able to focus on critical psychological tasks: "The relations are clarified because this modern family is 'stripped down' to what apparently approaches certain minimum structural and fundamental essentials," he wrote. Indeed, "the American family has been evolving into a new stability in which the emphasis is on the nuclear family."[12] Critical to this was what Parsons called "role differentiation," where wives/mothers took on the emotional tasks of gratification, warmth, and stability while husband/fathers focused on instrumental tasks in the outside world:

> If the nuclear family consists in a defined 'normal' complement of the male adult, female adult and their immediate children, the male adult will play the role of instrumental leader and the female adult will play the role of expressive leader.[13]

He acknowledged that this "companionship" or "companionate" family exacted a high emotional price from husband and wife, as they elaborated and refined their functional roles. Men served their families as chairman-of-the-board figures, looking outward. Women looked inward, focusing on "glamour patterns," "personal adornment," and the crafting of a pleasant home environment to ease psychological tensions.[14]

"Personality adjustment" toward these ends, Parsons insisted, became the core task of the companionate marriage of the 1950s.

Another figure in this school, William J. Goode, saw the whole world essentially adopting this model. Characterized by few productive tasks, weak ties to kin, high mobility, relatively high divorce, and "intense emotional" interaction, this structure marked the next step in global family evolution:

> Everywhere the ideology of the [companionate] family is spreading.... It appeals to the disadvantaged, to the young, to women, and to the educated.

It succeeded, he said, because of the close fit between this family form and the modern industrial system. Revealingly, though, in the year 1963 Goode also argued that the strong role differences between husbands and wives were more-or-less permanent:

> [W]e do not believe that any family system now in operation, or likely to emerge in the next generation, will grant full equality to women.

Why? Because:

> The family base upon which all societies rest at present requires that much of the daily work of the house and children be handed over to women.[15]

While seeming to affirm the traditional family, the narrow conception of family tasks in "companionate marriage" actually left families vulnerable. For example, federal policy came to favor the functionless home. Government housing agencies pushed designs that eliminated work rooms, pantries, large kitchens, sewing rooms, and parlors, to be replaced by functionless "open spaces." As urban planner John Dean explained in 1953, suburban homes should focus on maintaining "family interaction without recourse to the traditional housekeeping dwelling unit." Instead of designs "inherited from the family farm," homes should be built more in harmony with modern life patterns focused on psychological intimacy and consumption.[16] Architect Svend Reimer, writing in 1951, stressed that "housing attitudes must be related to long-term trends of social change in the family." They must evolve. In place of formal, single-purpose, and work rooms, suburban homes should have open, "flexible rooms that serve the every day life of the family and reduce household chores to the minimum." He concluded: "The goal of home construction lies in...a frictionless family life."[17] Similarly, federal education policy under the Smith-Lever and Smith-Hughes Acts, which had favored training in homemaking and homebuilding tasks from 1914 into the early 1950s, shifted curricula in favor of training girls in more ambiguous psychological tasks.

The Feminists Return

Alas, in 1963, Betty Friedan's *The Feminine Mystique* appeared. The book lashed out at the "companionate marriage" celebrated and defended by Parsons, Goode, and the other functionalists. Indeed, a conservative reading of Friedan's book is possible, as she exposes the weaknesses of the suburban life model. Some aspects of her argument even implied a return to an older, more agrarian family life. But in the end, Friedan herself turned out to be acolyte for social evolution. She simply argued that the functionalists wanted to have their evolutionary cake and to eat it, too.

Friedan pointed to the fatal inconsistencies in their argument. As she reported, Parsons himself had admitted:

> ...that the "domestic" aspect of the housewife role "has declined in importance to the point where it scarcely approaches a full-time occupation for the vigorous person"; that the "glamour pattern" is "inevitably associated with a rather early age level"...[and] "that in the adult feminine role there is quite sufficient strain and insecurity... [manifested] in the form of neurotic behavior"...

And still, Friedan complained, Parsons had the gall to insist that women adjust themselves to these fragile, disordered roles.

The suburbs, which Parsons praised as fitting homes for companionate families, drew her scorn. Friedan called them "ugly and endless sprawls," where women did "the time-filling busy work of suburban house and community." She blasted "the open plan" of most new suburban housing, "noisy" places without walls and doors, where the woman in her kitchen would never be without her children, and where the "one free-flowing room" created a continual mess.

However, rather than returning to an older model of family living, Friedan insisted on an elimination of the last remnants of economic cooperation in the home:

> [F]or the suburban and city housewife, the fact remains that more and more of the jobs that used to be performed in the home have been

taken away: canning, baking bread, weaving cloth and making clothes, educating the young, nursing the sick, taking care of the aged. It is possible [for women] to reverse history—or kid themselves that they can reverse it—by baking their own bread, but the law does not permit them to teach their own children at home....[18]

Instead, social evolution now pointed toward young mothers in the workplace, small children in day care, and an end to the traditional home.

So energized and directed, Friedan's book had a powerful impact. The equity feminist movement quickly gained strength and won important political victories through Title VII of the Civil Rights Act of 1964, which mandated sexual equality in employment practices, and Title IX of the Education Act of 1971, which did the same for schooling. Federal policy, which had already worked in the 1940s and 1950s to create economically functionless homes, now aimed at ending even the "division of labor" between husband and wife, as expressed through the recently favored "companionate" model.

Sexual Evolution

This evolutionary approach to the family also radically altered understanding of the "sexual" aspect of marriage; specifically, shifting its core meaning from "procreation" to "pleasure." Ogburn, again, was instrumental here. He emphasized the profound importance of the sharply falling American birthrate: "In 1930, for the first time there were fewer children under five years of age in one census year than in the one preceding." This presaged an emptying of schools and depopulation. More important for him, it pointed to a different kind of marriage:

> ...[T]here are many wives without children....In other families with only one or two children the mother devotes only a few years to child rearing. Families without children may almost be classed as a different type of family.

Indeed, Ogburn called for a fundamental reappraisal of the meaning of marriage:

> The relationship of husband and wife is clearly at the center of the problem of the modern family since most families have children with

them for only a part of married life or not at all and since so many other functions of the family have declined. The stability of the future family is not clearly seen.[19]

Ernest W. Burgess and Henry J. Locke, in their 1945 book *The Family*, agreed that as families shed their formal legal and economic functions, and shrank in size with fewer children, they reorganized around psychological tasks. This new step in social evolution rested on "mutual affection," "sympathetic understanding," and "comradeship," rather than procreation. The home now focused less on children and more on psychological intimacy and sexual love.[20]

Indeed, the "companionate marriage" elevated sex as a mode of self-definition. True, during the 1940s and 1950s, sexuality remained tied by popular mores and expert opinion to marriage. But as functional productive tasks and children diminished as the ends of marriage, these same experts urged men and women to reach for higher levels of sexual and emotional compatibility. Companionate marriage, the experts said, rested on passion, romantic affection, emotional intimacy, and "shared ecstasy," not children.[21]

Unwittingly, but clearly, this analysis fed directly into the sexual revolution of the 1960's. First came the separation of sex from procreation, an advance bolstered by introduction of the birth control pill in 1964. For a brief time, though, acceptable sex and marriage remained bound. The U.S. Supreme Court caught this spirit briefly in its 1965 *Griswold* v. *Connecticut* decision.[22] Within a few years, however, a new singles culture embracing sexual experimentation, a feminist movement affirming equality in pre-marital sex, and media attention to "swinging" and "wife-swapping" out in the suburbs combined to separate sex from marriage. The so-called "Population Bomb" scare during the late 1960s gave another radical imperative to change: children should be avoided in marriage altogether. "Motherhood: Who Needs It?" was the feature article in a September 1970, issue of *Look* magazine. Hope for the nation lay with those "younger-generation females" who recognized that "it can be more loving to children not to have them."[23] The "childless marriage," once deemed a true sadness, became the "child free" marriage, noble and forward looking. According to historian

Stephanie Coontz, the final step in the sexual revolution came in the 1970's, when "a gay movement questioned the exclusive definition of sexual freedom in terms of heterosexuality."[24]

In short, the evolutionary appearance of the diminished "companionate marriage"—one without economic function and one with the sexual function redefined from "procreative" to "pleasure seeking"—cleared the path for more claims to change; and eventually to demands for "gay marriage." Indeed, according to one scientist, due their "playful, creative character…[y]ou could say that homosexuals are at the pinnacle of human evolution."[25] And who can deny such superior humans their due?

Faith and Science

So what shall we make out of all this? Traditionalists of a religious bent might suggest turning to *Genesis* 1 and 2, where they see marriage cast as an immutable, unchanging aspect of God's creation, fixed from the beginning:

> So God created man in his own image, in the image of God he created him; male and female he created them. And God blessed them, and God said to them, "Be fruitful and multiply, and fill the earth and subdue it; and have dominion over the fish of the sea and over birds of the air and over every living thing that moves upon the earth".… Therefore a man leaves his father and mother and cleaves to his wife and they become one flesh.[26]

These passages affirm marriage as both heterosexual ("Be fruitful and multiply and fill the earth") and economic (the passage regarding "subdue" and "have dominion"). It might even be said that the author of *Genesis* seems to agree with Westermarck and Murdock.

What does evolutionary science actually teach? Far from agreeing with contemporary "gay marriage" advocates, Charles Darwin actually built classic evolutionary theory on the idea of "reproductive success." Since homosexuality was, by definition, sterile, the behavior stood as an obvious biological dead end: a "genetic aberration," Darwin labeled it.

Contemporary evolutionary scholars implicitly agree. Writing in *Science*, for example, paleo-anthropologist C. Owen Lovejoy argues that "the unique sexual and reproductive behavior of man"—not growth of the cortex or brain—"may be the sine qua non of human origin." The human "nuclear family" was not the product of, say, nineteenth-century bourgeois culture or twentieth century Levittown. Rather, the paleo-anthropological record shows that the pairing-off of male and female "hominids" into something very much like traditional marriage reaches back over three million years, to the time when our purported ancestors left the trees on the African savannah and started walking on two legs. As Lovejoy concludes,

> ...both advances in material culture and the Pleistocene acceleration in brain development are sequelae to [i.e., follow after] an already established hominid character system, which included intensified parenting and social relationships, monogamous pair bonding, specialized sexual-reproductive behavior, and bipedality. [This model] implies that the nuclear family and human sexual behavior may have their ultimate origin long before the dawn of the Pleistocene.[27]

Other new evidence supports this conclusion. A 2003 paper featured in *The Proceedings of the National Academy of Science* examines "skeletal size dimorphism" (that is, the difference in male and female size) in *Australopithecus afarensis*, a human ancestor from 3-4 million years ago. Among the apes and other mammals, sexual dimorphism is greatest when sexual coupling is random or where one male accumulates numerous females. Dimorphism is least when male and female pair off in monogamous bonds. Overturning earlier assessments, this new study finds that *Australopithecus* males and females were nearly the same size, no different than men and women today. According to the Kent State research team, this means that this human ancestor was monogamous, with male and female in a permanent pair bond, "a social complex including male provisioning driven by female choice."[28]

Ronald Immerman of Case Western Reserve University reports in a 2003 issue of the journal, *Evolutionary Psychology*, that from the very beginning, our distinctly human ancestors showed a unique reproductive strategy where a female exchanged sexual exclusivity for special provisioning by a male. "This sharing of resources from man-to-woman is a universal," Immerman reports. Again from the beginning of the human race, it appears that women chose men not on the basis of physical size, but because of male skills in provisioning and loyalty: that is, women have bonded to men who reliably returned to the cave, hut, or split level tract home with fresh meat or a good paycheck. In this monogamous order, promiscuity stands out as a disease, an evolutionary danger. At the same time, the ethnographic "data suggest an independent man (to) child affiliative bond which is part of *Homo sapiens*' bio-cultural heritage," one found no where in the animal kingdom. Immerman explains this trait, as well, by evolutionary selection. Besides looking for reliable providers, women "were simultaneously selecting for traits which would forge a social father: a man who would form attachments—bond—with his young and who would be psychologically willing to share resources with those young."[29]

It would certainly be going too far to say that modern evolutionary theory and the Book of *Genesis* have converged; significant differences remain over key matters such as timing. All the same, it would be fair to say that new research guided by evolutionary theory does agree with the author of *Genesis* that humankind, from our very origin as unique creatures on earth, has been defined by heterosexual monogamy involving long-term pair bonding (that is, marriage in a mother-father-child household) and resting on the special linkage of the reproductive and the economic, where two become one flesh. Science shows that the evolution of marriage occurred—but only once—3 to 4 million years ago when "to be human" came to mean "to be conjugal." All the other cultural variations surrounding marriage are mere details; "change" is the mark of cultural strengthening or weakening around a constant human model. And, rather than being the "pinnacle" of evolution, homosexuality and "gay marriage" emerge as obvious dead-ends. Such practices are by definition sterile and evolutionary theory—on its own terms—depends on reproductive success.

In the name of evolution, the campaign for "same-sex marriage" openly mocks the religious heritage of Western civilization. It ignores the hard-won lessons of human history. And it rejects the results of scientific inquiry, relying instead on sentiment to make its case. In all these ways, the campaign is radical, indeed. Just as recklessly, this same campaign will, if successful, also subvert the one trait—permanent heterosexual pair-bonding focused on reproduction and child rearing—which science points to as unique to human nature and vital to human success, even existence on Earth. Advocates for change here actually play with elemental fire.

A New Home Economics

What then about the functionless home? What shall we do with that place which the rise of industrial organization has stripped of economic activity?

Part of the answer is that the economic evolutionists, from Engels to Ogburn to Goode to Friedan, have simply been wrong about the status of the home economy. It is true that many functions once conducted in homes were torn away by industrial organization in the nineteenth and twentieth centuries, with disorienting results (more on that in chapter 6). And yet, much of this trauma—from the rise of public schooling in the 1850s to the building of "companionship" suburban homes in the 1950s—was driven by government engineering. Other choices could have been made.

Moreover, even in modern industrial nations, a vast amount of productive activity still occurs in households, albeit uncounted and unheralded. Australian economists now lead the way in documenting this truth. For example, Duncan Ironmonger of the University of Melbourne offers a good summary of continuing home-centered activities, including meal preparation, laundry and cleaning, shopping, various forms of child care, elder care, gardening, pet care, repairs and maintenance, transportation, and volunteer community work. Moreover, the author shows that the quality of these goods and services is often of higher value than that found in the marketplace (for example, compare the parental care of children to that found in a commercial daycare center). The problem is that all of these activities occur on a non-cash basis, so their "economic value"—so to speak—is unclear and easy to ignore. In response, Ironmonger has carefully calculated the shadow value produced by "household industries," through both labor and capital. For Australia in 1992, he reports this so-called Gross Household Product to be worth $341 billion, nearly equal to the economic value added by market production. Assuming rough so-cio-economic equivalence between the USA and Australia (which is reasonable in this case), the same figure for the United States would be a Gross Household Product of $10 trillion in 2006.[30]

What then about marriage? The traditionalist case points to the needed recovery of a cultural understanding of marriage as the union of the sexual (meaning the reproductive) and the economic, with an insistence that law rest on this human universal. In the short run, this would be vital to the defense of marriage at a time when it faces profound legal and cultural challenges, rooted in misguided evolution theory. In the long run, it would be essential to the very health, and survival, of a nation.

A second imperative would be more productive and more vital homes. There are several successful contemporary models; I focus here on one. The clue lies in that throwaway line from Betty Friedan, who said,

> It is possible [for women] to reverse history—or kid themselves that they can reverse it—by baking their own bread, but the law does not permit them to teach their own children at home.[31]

Well, that—at least—has now changed, through the grassroots behavior and political action of homeschoolers since the early 1970s. From a mere handful then, homeschooling families may now number 700,000; homeschooled children over two million. In home education, we see the broad productive home visibly reborn, and an important "lost family function" returned to its proper place. The educational effects are vast: homeschoolers are reinventing both American teaching and learning; and the children excel. By grade eight, according to a recent federal government study, these children are—on average—almost four years ahead of their public and private school counterparts. More important, though, these refunctionalized families also remake the very psychology of homes. They become beehives of activity: the evidence suggests that these families are more likely than non-homeschooling households to live in semi-rural locations, tend a vegetable garden, engage in simple animal husbandry, create home businesses, and turn to home births.

Regarding the latter, homeshooling families are also rebuilding the bond of marriage and procreative sexuality. One 1997 survey found 98 percent of homeschooling children to be in married couple households. The sexual division-of-labor in these homes was more pronounced: 52 percent of homeschoolers lived in two-parent families with only one parent in the workforce, compared to 19 percent nationwide. And these families were noticeably larger: with nearly twice as many children as the national average. Indeed, 62 percent of homeschooling families have three or more children, compared to 20 percent nationwide; a third of these homes have four or more children, compared to only 6 percent nationwide.[32] "Functional" and "prolific," it appears, still do go together, underscoring both the poetry and the power of that wonderful phrase, "and they become one flesh."

"Gay marriage" has gained a hearing, in part, because many see heterosexual marriage in the early twenty-first century as falling far short of the traditional standard binding the reproductive and the economic. Accordingly, any effort to rehabilitate the institution of marriage must not stop with legal bans on "gay marriage." It must also embrace true encouragements to the reconstruction of the function-rich and child-rich home.

Notes

1.   "Canada OKs Gay Marriage," *Seattle Post-Intelligencer* (June 18, 2003); at: *http://seattlepi.nwsource.com/national/127105_marriage18. html* (2/27/04).
2.   Jacqueline Murray, "Same-Sex Union: The Final Frontier of Marriage Evolution," *Toronto Globe and Mail* (June 27, 2003); at: *http://www. theglobeand mail.com/servlet/ArticleNews /TPPrint/LAC/20030627/ COMARRIAGE* (2/27/04).
3.   Virginia Postrel, "Hayek on Gay Marriage," *Boston Globe* (Jan. 11, 2004); at: *http://www.boston.com/news/globe/ideas/articles/2004/01/11/hayek_on_gay_marriage?mode...* (2/27/04).
4.   Ellen Goodman, "Ruling Shows Evolution of Gay Marriage," Detroit News (Nov. 21, 2003); at: *http://www.detnews.com/2003/editorial/0311/21/a13-330835.htm* (2/27/04).
5.   Edward Westermarck, *The History of Human Marriage: 5th Edition* (London: Macmillan, 1925): 26-37, 69-72.
6.   George Peter Murdock, *Social Structure* (New York: The Free Press, 1965 [1949]): 1-8.

7. William J. Goode, *World Revolution and Family Patterns* (New York: The Free Press of Glencoe, 1963): 3.
8. See: Lewis H. Morgan, *Ancient Society* (New York: Henry Holt, 1878).
9. Friedrich Engels, *The Origin of the Family, Private Property and the State, trans. Ernest Untermann* (Chicago: Charles H. Kerr, 1902): 24, 27, 80-82, 90-92, 99.
10. Arthur W. Calhoun, *A Social History of the American Family: From Colonial Times to the Present,* Vol. III (New York: Barnes & Noble, 1945 [1917]): 165-75.
11. *Recent Social Trends in the United States: Report of The President's Research Committee on Social Trends,* Vol. I (New York: McGraw-Hill, 1933): xliv, xlv, 661-92, 705-07.
12. Promotional text for Parsons and Bales, *Family, Socialization and Interaction Process*, found on Goode, *World Revolution and Family Patterns*, back cover.
13. Talcott Parsons and Robert F. Bales, *Family, Socialization and Interaction Process* (Glencoe, IL: The Free Press, 1958): 315, 341.
14. Talcott Parsons, "An Analytical Approach to the Theory of Social Stratification," in *Essays in Sociological Theory* (Glencoe, IL: The Free Press, 1949): p. 174.
15. Goode, *World Revolution and Family Patterns*, pp. 8-10, 368-69, 373.
16. John P. Dean, "Housing Design and Family Values," *Land Economics* 29 (May 1953): 128-41.
17. Svend Reimer, "Architecture for Family Living," *Journal of Social Issues* 7 (1951): 140-51.
18. Betty Friedan, *The Feminine Mystique* (New York: Dell Publishing, 1963): 122, 232-34.
19. *Recent Social Trends*, pp. xliv, 688, 707. Emphasis added.
20. Ernest W. Burgess and Henry J. Locke, *The Family* (New York: American Book Company, 1945): 651-72.
21. See: "Marriage…What's the Point?" at: *http://www.jaguarwoman. com/mmart127.html* (3/4/04).
22. *Eisenstadt* v. *Baird*, 495 U.S. 438, 453 (1972).
23. Betty Rollin, "Motherhood: Who Needs It?" *Look* (September 22, 1970): 15-17.
24. Stephanie Coontz, *The Way We Never Were: American Families and the Nostalgia Trap* (New York: Basic Books, 1992): 197.
25. Quotation from zoologist Clive Bromhall, in "Gay people the 'pinnacle of evolution,' study says," at *http://uk.gay.com/headlines/4882* (3/4/04).
26. *Genesis* 1: 27-28; 2: 24 (Revised Standard Version).

27. C. Owen Lovejoy, "The Origin of Man," *Science* 211 (Jan. 23, 1981): 348. Emphasis added.

28. Phillip L. Reno, Richard S. Meindl, Melanie A. McCollum, and C. Owen Lovejoy, "Sexual Dimorphism in Australopithecus afarensis was similar to modern humans," *Proceedings of the National Academy of Science* 100 (Aug. 5, 2003): 9404-09.

29. Ronald S. Immerman, "Perspectives on Human Attachment (Pair Bonding): Eve's Unique Legacy of a Canine Analogue," *Evolutionary Psychology* 1 (2003): 138-54.

30. Duncan Ironmonger, "Counting Outputs, Capital Inputs and Caring Labor: Estimating Gross Household Product," *Feminist Studies* 2 (1996): 37-64.

31. Friedan, The Feminine Mystique, p. 232.

32. "Homeschooling in the United States: 1999," National Center for Education Statistics, U.S. Department of Education; at *http://nces. ed.gov/pubs2001/HomeSchool/chara.asp.*

3

"Speak Now or Forever Hold Your Peace": The Communal Nature of Marriage

Confusion over the meaning of marriage has given new energy to the idea of "freedom to marry." The concept takes several forms. As one Massachusetts advocate of a pluralistic bent has phrased it, "the right to love and to celebrate our relationships, in whatever form they take, is a fundamental human right that should be protected."[1] As a Coloradan of a more libertarian persuasion puts it, "to be licensed by a bunch of bureaucrats for the most private and sacred act of marriage—that's demeaning. It's simply none of the government's business whom I marry."[2] Related takes on this concept include "The Marriage Resolution" put forward by the group appropriately called Freedom to Marry and recently advanced in San Francisco:

> "Because marriage is *a basic human right* and *an individual choice,* RESOLVED, the State should not interfere with same-gender couples who choose to marry and share fully and equally in the rights, responsibilities, and commitment of civil marriage.[3]

At most, in this view, the government's role is simply to register those couples freely entering civil marriage, so they might qualify for the benefits and public blessing involved.

My argument is that the appeal to freedom here is false and misleading. Rather than an expression of true liberty, the phrase, "Freedom to Marry" is "libertine" in effect, an invitation to social disorder. The "freedom to marry" idea presupposes that marriage is a private event, an arrangement by and for the couple. It presumes that marriage exists to recognize their love and promise of devotion to each other, to bless their companionship, but no more. The one promised public benefit, in this otherwise privatized and minimalist view of marriage, is reduced promiscuity by the sexual pair.

And yet, the very nature of the average wedding event belies such a narrow view of marriage. The boisterous celebration mounted, the gathering of kith and kin, of friends and neighbors, of former teachers and co-workers, and the feast spread out traditionally by the bride's parents: these testify to more than an end to promiscuity or public recognition of a love affair. The wedding is *a communal event*, where various levels of community find their own renewal and hope. Focusing only on the needs of the couple ignores the communitarian nature of true marriage and the claims of these others on each marriage.

In the traditional Christian wedding service, there was the time when the minister would pause and ask the congregation: "Does anyone here know a reason why this man and this woman should not be joined together? If so, speak now or forever hold your peace." This has been the moment which acknowledged the "community's" interest in the wedding, where persons could assert themselves to prevent a marriage that threatened broader relationships. It reminded the marrying couple, as well, that their vows were not only between themselves, but were also made with *concentric rings of others* holding as well a vested interest in the making and preservation of this marriage.

What are these concentric rings of others…of community? And why do they also have a claim on each true marriage? I will explore five: (1) the community of potential parents with their unborn children; (2) kin or extended family; (3) the neighborhood; (4) the community of faith; and (5) the nation as community.

The Community of Parents and Their Unborn Children

Grievous challenges to the institution of marriage are nothing new. The Soviet Bolsheviks waged war on marriage and home for the first two decades of the Russian Revolution, 1917-36. A century and a quarter earlier, the Jacobins of The French Revolution also sought to tear down marriage laws resting on traditional principles. The proposed French Civil Code of 1801, for example, promised "freedom to marry" and easy divorce. Ignoring both Christian thought and the evidence of all history, the radical authors of this measure argued that "what marriage itself is was previously unknown, and it is only in recent times that men have acquired precise ideas on marriage." Building on the thought of Jean-Jacques Rousseau, the architects of the 1801 Code urged that marriage be made "natural," by which they meant animalistic, subject to the ebb and flow of the passions. Marriage, as such, should be easy to enter and easy to leave.

Louis de Bonald, a statesman and a founder of modern social science, rose in defense of traditional marriage. His extraordinary 1801 book, titled in English translation *On Divorce*, remains a most valuable resource in helping sort out issues regarding marriage. It defends traditional marriage through an appeal to reason and the natural order.

Bonald's first task was to clarify "that marriage, in itself and at bottom, has always been a civil, religious, and physical act at once." He then set out to rescue the label, "natural," from the disciples of Rousseau. Marriage was, in fact, both divine and human, he said:

> …[I]t derives from the constitution of our being, of our nature, and is a natural act: for the true nature of man and the real constitution of his being consist in natural relationships with his being's author [i.e., God], and in natural relationships, both moral and physical, with his fellows.[4]

Marriage attracted the attention of civil legislators, in Bonald's view, because it was "the founding act of domestic society, whose interests should be guaranteed by civil authority." But this domestic society did not really rest on the needs or desires of the spouses: "the end of marriage is…*not* the happiness of the spouses, if by happiness one understands an idyllic pleasure of the heart and senses." Rather:

> [T]he end of marriage is the *reproduction* and, above all, the *conservation* of man, since this conservation cannot, in general, take place outside of marriage, or without marriage.

By "conservation," Bonald meant the care, rearing, education, and protection of children, which he believed could occur successfully only in the married-couple home.

If pleasure or happiness was the goal of marriage, then the civil authority had no business being involved. Instead:

> [P]olitical power *only* intervenes in the spouse's contract of union because it represents the unborn child, *which is the sole object of marriage*, and because it accepts the commitment made by the spouses in its presence and under its guarantee *to bring that child into being.*

In effect, a marriage "is truly a contract between three persons, two of whom are present, one of whom (the [potential] child) is absent, but is represented by public power, guarantor of the commitment made by the two spouses to form a society."

This also explained why civil marriage was restricted to heterosexual pairs: "Political power cannot guarantee the stability of the domestic persons without knowing them; hence, the necessity of the civil act, which makes known the commitment of the man and woman, and of the birth certificate, which makes known the father, mother, and child." Bonald understood that public policy on marriage must be built on this *ideal* family structure, and not on some lowest common denominator "of the heart and the senses."

Bonald also explained why the marriage of a man and a woman who proved infertile, or unable to create a child, remained valid. Many of the French Revolution's philosophers worried about the size of the French population, and called for easy divorce in cases of failed fertility so that new pairings of men and women might be tried to produce the needed children for war. Bonald replied:

> …whatever importance may be attached to population by these great depopulators of the universe; they would doubtless not dare to maintain that in human marriages one should, as on stud farms, proceed by trial.

In short, government should not be in the business of fertility tests. Rather, it should understand the potential fertility of all male-female bonds (perhaps even modern ones via the Petri dish) and the powerful positive effects on children of the complementarity of man and woman. The state then holds together the potential or actual parents for the sake of good "conservation" of the potential or actual child.[5]

Extended Family, or Kin

Each marriage is also a covenant between the couple and their kin. In marriage, two families merge in a manner that perpetuates and invigorates both. It is true that issues of property are not as prevalent in a wedding today as they were, say, 500 years ago. But the great chain of being, binding the living to ancestors and to posterity, remains as important as ever. Every wedding of young people forges a new link in that chain, for the family's future still rests in their potential fertility. Even today, family members will travel great distances to attend the wedding of a cousin, nephew, or niece, still acknowledging the importance of both the promise and the event itself to their own identity and continuity. As President Theodore Roosevelt once wrote, a people existed only as its "sons and daughters thought of life not as something concerned only with the selfish evanescence of the individual, but as a link in the great chain of creation and causation [forged by] the vital duties and the high happiness of family life."[6] Indeed: "the great chain of creation and causation" over the generations appeared, link by link, through new marriage.

Marriage also serves as the natural solution to human society's dependency problem. Just as marriage brings forth and cares for new life, it also creates bonds and obligations that provide care for the very old, the weak, and the infirm. In a society with a culture of true marriage, these tasks fall on kin networks, where the aged or disabled can receive care, purpose, and respect; and where kin insure that no family member falls through the extended family's safety net. It is again the chain of fertility—child, parent, grandparent, blood kin—that brings to fruition these natural sentiments of intergenerational care. Where a culture of marriage fails, these tasks pass to the public purse, to government, at huge expense.

Indeed, a common goal of the contemporary women's movement and modern socialism has been to replace the bonds of marriage and kin with a universal dependence on the welfare state. The feminist analyst Carol Pateman argues that women's growing dependence on the state is a logical corollary to feminist goals, and a stimulus to state entitlements as a substitute for family-centered care. Frances Piven stresses the "large and important relationship" of women to the welfare state as direct employees of its program, noting that nearly three-quarters of government welfare jobs are held by women. Put another way: less true marriage means more government.[7]

The Community of the Neighborhood

Neighbors and friends also have a deep interest in nurturing and preserving true marriage. For some reason, this attribute of marriage seems best captured by fiction and poetry. I still recall a powerful telling of this truth by the National Public Radio humorist Garrison Keillor. About twenty years ago, during the first—and in my opinion the best—iteration of his show, *Prairie Home Companion*, he told the story of receiving a letter from an old friend, now a professor of sociology at a Midwestern college. This friend was married and had several small children; but on the spring day recorded, he was sitting on the front porch of his home, going for the weekend to a sociologists' convention in a nearby city. Picking him up in her convertible would be the newest member of the department, a beautiful young woman with a new Ph.D. They had flirted with each other over the prior few months and "the sweet prospects of adultery" that weekend were on his mind. But as he sat, waiting for her to arrive, he heard his wife's voice as she cared for the baby and saw his young son playing with the children next door. And he saw his neighbors at work in their yards or playing catch with their own children. The web of relationships in his neighborhood broke into his mind with a burning clarity. His quest for pleasure, he recognized, would not only rip through his own marriage and home, but through this neighborhood, shattering friendships, creating doubts and fears in children, tearing apart the bonds of responsibility and care that surrounded a people living in one place. His faithlessness would affect not only his wife and children, but in a way *all* wives and *all* children. Stung by this revelation, he stood up, lifted his suitcase, walked inside, kissed his startled wife, and unpacked his bag.

The Kentucky poet Wendell Berry, in his collection *A Timbered Choir: The Sabbath Poems*, underscores how each couple on their wedding day renew their place on earth, their community:

Again, hope dreams itself
Awake. The year's first lambs
Cry in the morning dark.
And, after all, we have
A garden in our minds.

We living know the worth
Of all the dead have done
Or hoped to do. We know
That hearts, against their doom
Must plight an ancient troth.

Now come the bride and groom,
Now come the man and woman
Who must begin again
The work divine and human
By which we live on earth.[8]

Berry explains that the bride and groom "say their vows to the community as much as to one another, and the community gathers around them to hear and to wish them well, on their behalf and on its own."[9] In his wonderful short story, "A Jonquil for Mary Penn," Berry uses a rural Kentucky setting to explain how a young marriage merges into a neighborhood:

[O]n rises of ground or tucked into folds were the grey, paintless buildings of the farmsteads, connected to one another by lanes and paths. Now [Mary Penn] thought of herself as belonging there, not just because of her marriage to Elton but also because of the economy that the two of them had made around themselves and their neighbors. She had learned to think of herself as living and working at the center of a wonderful provisioning:...the little commerce of giving and taking that spoked along paths *connecting her household to the others.*[10]

And in a poem addressed to his wife, Tanya, on their thirty-first anniversary, the poet illuminates how their marriage encompasses "many others"—neighbors, friends, kin, and posterity:

Another year has returned us
to the day of our marriage
thirty one years ago. Many times
we have known, and again forgot

in our cruel separateness,
that making touch that feelingly
persuades us what we are:
one another's and many others....

How strange to think of children
yet to come, into whose making we
will be made, who will not know us
even so little as we know
ourselves, who have already gone
so far beyond our own recall.[11]

Marriage and its fruit, children, bind us to neighborhood, space, and time, giving substance to our loyalties toward "a place on earth." Berry writes:

Come into the dance of the community, joined
in a circle, hand in hand, the dance of the eternal love
of women and men for one another
and of neighbors and friends for one another.[12]

The Community of Faith

In Western Europe before the Reformation, governments were not usually engaged in the registration and regulation of marriage. This was left to the One, Holy, and Catholic Christian Church, centered in Rome. Church marriage courts handled disputes and considered cases for potential annulment. With marriage deemed a sacrament, grounded in Divine mystery, divorce was an impossibility. In nations, and *then* a civilization, with only one recognized church, this structure worked reasonably well.

The Protestant movement of the sixteenth century shook the system to its core. On the one hand, the Reformers argued that there was no Biblical warrant for considering marriage a Christian sacrament and—where they held sway—abolished church marriage courts. They also reasoned that the Gospel text allowed for divorce in cases of adultery, with remarriage possible for the offended spouse. On the other hand, they said that marriage was a *spiritual* bond superior to all other natural arrangements, including the celibacy practiced by the Catholic priesthood and in holy orders.

In Martin Luther's words, marriage was the highest of estates, "the real religious order on earth," divinely ordained, "pleasing to God and precious in his sight." The Reformers called on rulers to govern marriage through Biblical principles and to punish those who offended Christian morality.[13] And for three or four centuries, one could conclude that their system also worked reasonably well.

Still, as one Catholic writer, R.V. Young, has summarized, Protestantism enhanced marriage in social status and "as a means of personal companionship and individual, earthly happiness, but in desacramentalizing it, lowered its resistance to the pressures of the secular world."[14]

Indeed, strains and disorders were evident by the middle decades of the nineteenth century. In Britain and America, for example, divorce had remained rare until then. A special act of Parliament, or by a state legislature in America, had been required for divorce, underscoring the grave and rare natures of the act. Yet a great loosening of divorce laws began around 1850, as the process was transferred to civil courts.

In the twentieth century, this disorder fed into the "no-fault" divorce revolution of the 1960s and 1970s. Despite changes during the prior century, until then the notion of "fault-based" divorce had still underscored the public nature of marriage. Adultery, desertion, or cruelty had to be proved. This institution was still something larger that the will and emotions of the spouses; the public interest dictated that "fault" be determined, before society would relinquish its claims on the couple's vow. Indeed, divorce still had something of the quality of a crime against the social order. But as the American states embraced "no fault," they unwittingly destroyed the last remnants of the Protestant scheme: that is, the expectation that rulers and judges would govern marriage by Christian principles, broadly defined.

All the same, the issue has not yet died. The "covenant marriage" movement of the last decade has sought, with some success, to restore to law elements of both the public interest in marital stability and religious covenantal thinking. More directly, some individuals have begun to challenge the "no fault" divorce regime as a violation of religious liberty; or, put another way, as a violation of the implicit agreement reached between church and state back in the sixteenth century. Specifically, in September, 2000, I testified as an expert witness in Harris County, Texas, Family Court in the case of *Waite* v. *Waite*. Here, the wife, Margaret Waite, had filed unilaterally for divorce, claiming under the 1970 Texas "no fault" statute that she had "irreconcilable differences" with her husband which destroyed "the legitimate ends of the marital relationship." However, husband Daniel Waite objected to the divorce, arguing that the 1970 law had abrogated the Christian principle of covenant marriage and had so violated *his* religious liberty. Eighty-seven percent of persons marry in churches, he argued. In assuming authority to govern marriages, the state of Texas also took on the duty to protect the covenantal religious nature of the bond. "No fault" divorce violated that obligation.[15]

Despite my own best efforts on the witness stand, the family court judge denied Mr. Waite's claims. He took the case to an Appeals Court, where he again lost. This time, though, the vote on the three judge panel was 2 to 1. That is, one Appeals Justice—Kem Thompson Frost—agreed with Mr. Waite's contention that the state had an obligation to protect the religious covenant in marriage, and that "no fault" divorce violated the religious liberty provision of the Texas Constitution. This was, in a way, a legal breakthrough. More may be heard from this argument in the future.

Some now argue, as well, that marriage should be completely privatized: that government should get out of the matrimony business, and return the process to religion. Well, this could work if the United States had one church—as in Medieval Europe—and granted that church the police powers needed to enforce its rulings in the inevitable disputes. Or "privatization" could work if the government agreed to enforce the disparate marital rules of each religious faith on its members: 'Indissoluble marriage' among Roman Catholics; up to four wives among Muslims; temple marriages for all eternity among the Mormons; divorce only for the victims of adultery among the Lutherans (after which, Martin Luther actually recommended executing the former spouse who had committed the adultery); and creative divorce among the Unitarians. Or "privatization" could work if marriage was stripped of all legal, economic, and social status, existing merely as a symbolic act of friendship. But the first two possibilities are, quite frankly, impossible in the current American context. And the third possibility would undo the very essence of marriage, making the whole exercise moot. This "privatization" idea, I believe, can be safely cast aside.

The Nation as Community

The nation also has a claim on the marital pair. Simply put, the future of every people comes through the cradles found in married-couple homes. The case of the European peoples is instructive here, where a dramatic decline in fertility since 1970 has been accompanied by—even led by—a fall in the marriage rate. Consider, for example, these representative nations:

	Total First Marriage Rate*			Total Fertility Rate**		
	Prior Year		2003	%	1970-75	2000-2005	% Change
Ireland	1.04	(1974)	.59	-43%	3.8	1.9	-50%
Italy	.97	(1974)	.61	-31%	2.3	1.2	-48%
Spain	1.01	(1974)	.59	-42%	2.9	1.2	-59%
Norway	.80	(1975)	.54	-33%	2.2	1.8	-18%
Australia	.78	(1976)	.60	-23%	2.5	1.7	-32%
Canada	.81	(1975)	.64	-21%	2.0	1.5	-25%

*The total first marriage rate, on the left, estimates the proportion of women who would have ever married by age 50 if age-specific first marriage rates in a given year applied throughout life. A figure of 1.0 suggests that all members of a generation would marry. Since this rate is sensitive to changes in the timing of marriage, it may exceed 1.0 in certain years.

**The Total Fertility Rate calculates the average number of children born per woman over the course of a generation if age specific fertility rates in a given year applied over their whole reproductive lives. A figure of 2.1 just insures the replacement of a population.

These numbers show that, as traditional marriage fades, there will be a paucity of children and a diminished nation. The retreat from true marriage and the retreat from children go together. Also, if the children that are born appear outside of traditional marriage, their prospects for productive lives sharply diminish, just as the odds that they will become public charges—as welfare recipients or as prisoners—grow. These facts of household life are now indisputable, and give support to a preferential option for traditional marriage by the nation-state, be it evidenced through marriage-sensitive tax provisions, welfare policy, or simple marriage law.

This was, of course, once understood in this land. As the U.S. Supreme Court put the matter back in 1888, in its famed *Maynard* decision, marriage is

> ...something more than a mere contract. It is an institution, in the maintenance of which in its purity the public is deeply interested, for it is the foundation of society.[16]

A century later, though, the Court has grown strangely blind to this deep national interest. The dismissal of marriage in *Eisenstadt v. Baird* is consistent with the logic of no-fault divorce, which also denies the public's interest in wedlock.

Indeed, it is through an analysis of divorce that we can better understand the public nature of marriage. After all, divorce is merely the backside of marriage. Legally, the marital covenant is only as strong as the provisions which govern an exit from its terms.

It seems useful to note here that "no fault" divorce is actually no new idea, nor some inevitable result of social evolution or modernity. Rather, it seems to be a standing temptation for any society or era. For men, at least, "no-fault" was the rule in Old Testament times. Much later, a forceful advocate for "no fault" was none other than the great seventeenth-century English poet, John Milton. Predictably, his views were shaped by his own troubled marriage. In 1642, when he was thirty-four years of age, Milton traveled to Oxfordshire to confer on a debt owed to his father by one Richard Powell. A month later, Milton returned to his London home with a bride, seventeen-year-old Mary Powell, daughter of the debtor. The marriage quickly developed problems: a husband twice the age of his wife; a young bride who missed her boisterous childhood home; and political differences. Civil War was about to descend on England: the Powells were staunchly Royalist, while the Miltons stood for Parliament. After Mary went back for a visit with her parents, she refused to return to her husband.

Milton grew enraged. He authored four pamphlets on divorce, arguing for quick dissolution of a marriage on the grounds of incompatibility and for a right to remarry. Sounding like a modern advocate for "Freedom to Marry," Milton took a minimalist view of marriage's purpose: "in God's intention a meet and happy conversation is the chiefest and noblest end of marriage." Wedlock existed to make people happy by dispelling loneliness through companionship. If unhappiness resulted, the union should be dissolved: "Love in marriage cannot live or subsist, unless it be mutual; and where love cannot be, there can be left of wedlock nothing, but the empty husk of an outside matrimony." Indeed, he said, there was a moral duty to terminate an empty marriage. And the state must not interfere, for "to interpose a jurisdictive power upon the inward and irremediable disposition of man, to command love and sympathy, to forbid dislike against the guiltless instinct of nature, is not within the province of any law to reach."[17]

As a postscript, I note that Mary did finally return to her husband in 1645 and they found a certain happiness. Moreover, John Milton would rescue his in-laws from impoverishment after the Royalist cause in Oxfordshire was crushed by the armies of Parliament. So true marriage works, to bind up the wounds and heal the divisions even of nations torn by civil war.

It is also possible to *calculate*, using hard numbers, the nation's profound interest in marriage if we use the negative calculus of divorce.

To begin with, we know that one measurable cost of "no-fault" divorce has been more divorce. Advocates of this change during the 1960s and 1970s always claimed that their goal was simply to remove acrimony from the divorce process, for the good of all concerned. Divorce rates were already climbing and, in the words of one prominent sociologist, "the adoption of no-fault divorce was a late and largely redundant step in the lowering of moral, social, and legal barriers to divorce." However, more careful research analyzing divorce trends in thirty-four states for the ten years before and after the introduction of "no fault," found that this legal innovation "contributed directly to more divorce or sooner divorces than would have happened otherwise." The researchers even calculate that "57,000 extra divorces" occur each year in the U.S. due directly to the no-fault revolution.[18]

Second, we can also count the effects of divorce on children, Bonald's "third party" in the marriage that the states no longer really protect. Specifically:

- The children of divorce have significantly more health problems than children in intact homes.[19]
- The children of divorce have much higher incidences of depression, fear of abandonment, and delinquency.[20]
- The children of divorce are more likely to drop out of high school and less likely to graduate from college than are children in intact homes, even when compared to families losing a father through death.[21]
- And the children of divorce are more likely to engage in premarital sex at a young age, to become parents before marriage, and to need psychological help.[22]

Of course, the costs imposed by divorce on young lives can never adequately be added up. Who can put a value on the diminished hopes of even one child's life? However, it turns out that we can put a dollar figure on the costs of divorce that accrue to the public at large. Economist David Schramm shows in a 2003 study that divorce imposes a heavy financial burden on all taxpayers. Direct costs to the state of Utah include increased Medicaid expenses, child support enforcement, funds for Temporary Assistance to Needy Families (TANF), food stamps, and public housing assistance. Indirect costs include increased incarceration in prisons, more elderly persons without spousal support, and greater illegal drug use. Using careful (and probably low) assumptions, Schramm calculates that "the 'average' divorce costs state and federal governments $30,000." In a given year, the total is $33.3 billion for the nation as a whole, or $312 for each American household. In crude, materialistic terms, this public cost of divorce underscores the profound social interest in marriage.[23]

In sum, marriage is a social and communal, rather than a private, event. Alongside the marital couple, it engages at least five levels of community: the unborn or potential children; extended family or kin; the neighborhood; the religious communion; and the nation. This civil institution exists for the propagation of children and for their "conservation" through nurture, education, and protection. Only the union of man and woman can properly fulfill both of these tasks. Public policy toward marriage must assume and build on this ideal structure, rather than on some lowest common denominator of the passions. All five levels of community have a deep and compelling interest in the formation and preservation of true marriages. And the wise government lifts up obstacles and checks on divorce, for its real costs will fall on vulnerable children and the community at large.

So-called "same-sex" marriages trivialize the true institution, for these unions are unable to meet the two ends of marriage: the propagation and conservation of children. Concerning propagation, these pairings are sterile by definition. When they do claim children, it is usually through either the trauma of divorce or the unnatural and sometimes dangerous manipulation of the laboratory. Moreover, these pairings cannot effect proper conservation of children, for again by definition they exclude either man or woman, so denying the complementarity of the sexes on which the good nurturing home rests.

And so, on that day when an Episcopalian priest in a Massachusetts' church intones "If anyone present knows a reason why this man and man [or woman and woman] should not be joined together, speak now or forever hold your peace"....The proper response is: "I do."

Notes

1. "Libertarian Activist [David Rostcheck] Files 'Freedom of Marriage' and 'Freedom of the Bedroom' Legislation," Dec. 18, 1998; at http://www.lpma.org/releases/981218.htm [2/04/04].
2. Ari Armstrong, "Get Government Out of Marriage," *Colorado Freedom Report,* at http://www.freecolorado.com/2004/01/nogovmarriage.html [2/04/04].
3. "The Marriage Resolution," at http://www.freedomtomarry.org/marriage_resolution.asp [2/04/04].
4. Louis de Bonald, *On Divorce* [1801], trans. and ed. by Nicholas Davidson (New Brunswick, NJ: Transaction Publishers, 1992): 36-37.
5. De Bonald, *On Divorce,* pp. 63-64, 175. Emphasis added.

6.   Theodore Roosevelt, *The Works of Theodore Roosevelt: Memorial Edition,* Vol. XXI (New York: Charles Scribner's Sons, 1924): 263.

7.   Carol Pateman, "The Patriarchal Welfare State," in Amy Gutman, ed., *Democracy in the Welfare State* (Princeton, NJ: Princeton University Press, 1988): 231-60; and Frances Fox Piven, "Ideology and the State: Women, Power, and the Welfare State," in Linda Gordon, ed., *Women, the State and Welfare* (Madison: University of Wisconsin Press, 1990): 251-64.

8.   Wendell Berry, *A Timbered Choir: The Sabbath Poems,* 1979-1997 (Washington, DC: Counterpoint, 1998): 153.

9.   Wendell Berry, *Sex, Economy, Freedom & Community* (New York and San Francisco: Pantheon Books, 1992, 1993): 120-21, 133.

10. Wendell Berry, "A Jonquil for Mary Penn," in *Fidelity: Five Stories* (New York and San Francisco: Pantheon Books, 1992): 74-75.

11. Berry, *A Timbered Choir,* p. 99.

12. Wendell Berry, *Entries: Poems* (Washington, DC: Counterpoint, 1997): 40.

13. *Luther's Works,* Vol. 45 (Philadelphia: Muhlenburg Press, 1962): 18, 39-42, 154-55; and Stephen Ozment, *When Fathers Ruled: Family Life in Reformation Europe* (Cambridge, MA: Harvard University Press, 1980): 1-2, 100-19.

14. In Glenn W. Olsen, ed., *Christian Marriage: A Historical Study* (New York: Herder & Herder, 2001): 274.

15. *Waite v. Waite,* District Court, Harris, Texas, Trial Court Cause #99-48049 (September 18, 2000): 13-15.

16. *Maynard v. King,* 125 U.S. 190, 210-11 (1888).

17. John Milton, *Complete Prose Works of John Milton,* Vol. 2 (New Haven, CT: Yale University Press, 1959): 244-46, 254-58, 277-78, 346.

18. Joseph Lee Rodgers, Paul A. Nakonezny, and Robert D. Shull, "The Effect of No-Fault Legislation on Divorce: A Response to a Reconsideration," *Journal of Marriage and the Family* 59 (1997): 1026-30.

19. Jane Mauldon, "The Effect of Marital Disruption on Children's Health," *Demography* 27 (August 1990): 431-46.

20. Judith Wallerstein and Joan B. Kelly, *Surviving the Breakup: How Children and Parents Cope With Divorce* (New York: Basic Books, 1996): 46-50, 211; and Ronald L. Simons, et. al., "Explaining the Higher Incidence of Adjustment Problems Among Children of Divorce Compared with Those in Two-Parent Families," *Journal of Marriage and Family* 61 (Nov. 1999): 1020-33.

21. Timothy J. Biblarz and Greg Gottainer, "Family Structure and Children's Success: A Comparison of Widowed and Divorced Single-Mother Families," *Journal of Marriage and the Family* 62 (May 2000): 533-48.

22. K.E. Kiesnan and J. Habcraft, "Parental Divorce During Childhood:
     Age at First Intercourse, Partnership and Parenthood," *Population Stud-
     ies* 51 (1997): 41-55; and Teresa M. Cooney and Jane Kurz, "Mental
     Health Outcomes Following Recent Parental Divorce: The Case of
     Young Adult Offspring," *Journal of Family Issues* 17 (July 1996):
     495-513.
23. David Schramm, "What Could Divorce Be Costing Your State? The
     Costly Consequences of Divorce in Utah: The Impact on Couples,
     Communities, and Government," A Preliminary Report, 25 June 2003,
     Publication in Process, Department of Family, Consumer, and Human
     Development, Utah State University, Logan, Utah.

4

Standing for Liberty: Marriage, Virtue, and the Political State

A decade ago, I was speaking in Switzerland before a presumed friendly audience of psychologists, teachers, and physicians. My topic was the family as "the natural and fundamental...unit of society," a phrase found in the Universal Declaration of Human Rights, which seemed to be safe ground. In this talk, I made a positive reference to family policy involving state support for traditional marriages and children. As the question time started, though, a clearly agitated woman rose and asked me how I could endorse such an approach. "These are Nazi ideas," she declared.

Indeed, this fearful perception of "family policy" as fascist in inspiration is widespread in Europe. As a friend of mine who sits in Sweden's Parliament explains, "To favor the traditional family over here is to open oneself to the charge of being a Nazi." This attitude has, I believe, crippled contemporary European efforts to confront the continent's "birth dearth" and the gloomy twenty-first-century reality of depopulation. At the same time, the current push throughout the Western world for "same-sex marriage" rests on an often heard, similar argument. To oppose the "gay right" to marry is also to align oneself with the Nazis who persecuted homosexuals in the death camps of World War II.

My argument is that these views have the facts largely reversed. Rather than seeking stronger families, Nazi policy aimed at destroying family autonomy. Rather than affirming the traditional roles of husband and wife, of mother and father, Nazism sought a radical change in gender roles. Moreover, the relationship between

Nazism and homosexuality turns out to have been more complex than commonly supposed. More broadly, I will show why other totalitarian regimes have also sought to destroy marriage, both the "hard" regimes of the Soviet Union and Communist China and the "soft" totalitarianism of modern Democratic Socialism. And finally, I will explain why the true role of traditional marriage and family is that of standing for liberty.

The Nazi Family System

Turning to Germany, it is true that shortly after taking power in 1933, the National Socialist German Workers Party—or the Nazis—implemented a vast marriage incentive program. This included an interest-free loan to newlyweds of 1,000 Reich Marks (worth about a fifth of an average worker's annual salary) provided that the new wives would not work and that the couples could prove that they had no immediate Jewish ancestors. The money could be used only for the purchase of household goods, and 25 percent of the loan's principle would be forgiven on the birth of each child. The government also imposed a "bachelor tax" on the unmarried, rising to 5 percent of income. Moreover, the income tax allowed a deduction of 15 percent per child; parents with six or more children paid no income tax at all. The state outlawed birth control devices and stiffened penalties on abortionists. Gertrude Scholtz-Klink became *Reichsfrauenführerin*, or leader of all Nazi Women, in 1934 (and I assure the reader that Scholtz-Klink is her real name, not some parody of television's *Hogan's Heroes*). She developed other programs to encourage early marriage, homemaking wives, and motherhood. This is the "Nazi family policy" scorned by many Europeans today.

And yet, just beneath the surface lay a very different agenda, one that would emerge only with time. Anti-Semitism would be the only common plank. The best source here, in my opinion, is the 1987 book, *Mothers in the Fatherland: Women, the Family, and Nazi Politics*. Authored by the feminist historian Claudia Koonz, the book opens with a summary of her astonishing interview with Frau Scholtz-Klink. It turns out that this top woman Nazi was still very much alive in 1981, when Koonz was doing her research. And

Frau Scholtz-Klink was still very much a Nazi. While other top Nazi officials, after falling to the Allies in 1945, faced either a trial at Nuremberg or active deNazification, female Nazi leaders were simply ignored, left to go their own ways. Frau Scholtz-Klink told her stunned feminist American guest that she "had grown up in an anti-Semitic family, so the ideas did not seem so unusual." Other comments included: "Göring, Rosenberg, Hitler, Himmler…You can't imagine what gentlemen they all were"; and "If you could have seen the women of Berlin defending their city with their lives against the Russians, then you would believe how deeply German women loved our Führer."[1]

Koonz's subsequent investigation reveals the truths of Nazi family policy. As the historian summarizes: "Far from honoring the family, Scholtz-Klink used it as an invasion route into ordinary people's ethical choices, emotional commitments, and social priorities." Where traditionalist German women "viewed the family as an emotional 'space' and bulwark against the invasion of public life," Nazi women used the family to give the party "access to every German's most personal values and decisions."[2]

The Nazi Party actually cared nothing about the "happy home." Indeed, one goal was to destroy family autonomy, among party members and enemies of the party alike. As Koonz explains,

Nazi policy aimed at eroding family ties among victims and also among its own "Aryan" followers. In both cases, the goal was the same: to break down individual identity and to render people susceptible to whatever plans Hitler announced: eugenic breeding schemes for the chosen "Aryans" and genocide for the selected. Nazi guards [in the death camps] sent "men to the left" and "women to the right" for the same reasons they sent girls to the BDM [League of German Girls] and "Aryan" boys to The Hitler Youth…[C]ontrary to rhetoric praising the "strong family," [they divided up German society] to weaken family bonding and enhance total loyalty to the Führer.[3]

Indeed, authentic defenders of the family in Germany often stood as quiet opponents of the Nazi regime. For example, in the early 1930s, the largest woman's group in Germany was the Bund Deutsche Frauen (or The Federation of German Women's Organizations), embracing 500,000 members. The group, which had both Christian and Jewish members, held that "woman is the born guardian of human life," committed itself to the defense of infant life, and supported a family wage for fathers so that the employed mother might "quit her job and devote all her energies to motherhood." When ordered in May 1933 to submit to Nazification, the Federation voted instead to shut down. Even the rise in Germany's marriage rate during the 1930s may have had nothing to do with Nazi policy. To the contrary, there is evidence that marriage had actually become an anti-Nazi act. As Koonz conjectures, "Germans who drove the marriage rates upward may well have sought an escape from participation in the Nazified public square."[4]

Indeed, as the Nazi regime unfolded, it became clear that marriage was slated for elimination. Koonz again: "The war accelerated Hitler's determination to establish an entirely new social order based on race and sex, with the ideal couple at its core: not a husband and wife, but a soldier and his mother, obedient to Hitler, the patriarch über alles." The regime wanted racially pure babies, not frolicking, independent families, and the model for the new order was the *Lebensborn* home. In his book *Mein Kampf*, Hitler had described his vision of a nation guided by elite, black-uniformed troops obedient to the Führer alone and living in their own world. Heinrich Himmler created this elite as the SS and he urged his troops "to father as many children as possible without marrying." Women would live as brood mothers in eugenic convents (*Zuchtkloster*), served by pure-blooded Aryan SS stud-males (*Ehehelfer*). As Himmler explained in October, 1939:

> The greatest gift for the widow of a man killed in battle is always the child of the man she has loved. SS men and mothers of these children...show that you are ready, through your faith in the Führer and for the sake of the life of our blood and people, to regenerate life for Germany, just as bravely as you know how to fight and die for Germany.[5]

By early 1945, over 11,000 children sired by SS troops lived in *Lebensborn* homes; Himmler called them his greatest gift to the German nation.

Beneath this quest for children, though, lay a darker reality, at which Koonz only hints. Referring to Himmler's command to the SS ranks that they sire out-of-wedlock children, she concludes:

The order exposed the underlying axiom of all Nazi policy on the Woman Question: Women performed only one function, breeding the children who would be raised by the Reich as the soldiers and mothers of the next generation…. Promiscuity within an elite movement, like chastity in a religious order, maintains men's loyalty to a masculine corps and inhibits the formation of deep ties to women and children.[6]

"A Common Vice"?

As it turns out, Nazi promiscuity was apparently not only of the heterosexual kind. The question of homosexuality in the Nazi Party is a contentious one. As noted before, the dominant view today is that the Nazis ruthlessly suppressed homosexuals, symbolized by the "pink triangles" worn by accused homosexuals in the death camps. The contemporary play *Bent* shows a homosexual prisoner "trading up" his pink triangle for a yellow Jewish star to improve his status in the camp. Indisputable facts, such as the flagrant pederasty of Ernst Röhm, founder and leader of the SA Storm Troopers (or "brownshirts"), and his chief lieutenants are explained away as peculiarities of the early Nazi Party, eliminated by the Purge of 1934, the "Night of the Long Knives."[7]

In 1995, Scott Lively and Kevin Abrams published the book, *The Pink Swastika*. Inspired by the 1945 work of Samuel Igra, *Germany's National Vice*,[8] Lively and Abrams describe "the homoerotic" foundations of Nazi militarism. Their thesis is that "the National Socialist revolution and the Nazi Party were animated and dominated by militaristic homosexuals, pederasts, pornographers, and sado-masochists."[9]

This book generated howls of protest from the contemporary "gay community," including several websites designed solely to refute its argument. And the book does have a number of real limitations. Neither author appears to have had professional training as an historian, and their conclusions frequently jump well ahead of the facts. Most of their sources are secondary in nature; that is, the authors have not reviewed the primary documents. And the volume is published by an obscure press without the full tools of scholarship.

64   Conjugal America

All the same, Lively and Abrams pull together a good deal of material, some familiar to this historian and some new. When confirmed by other, independent, and reliable sources, their case rings at least partially true.

For example, they trace the common roots and parallel development of the early German "homosexual rights" campaign and the proto Nazi Party to a hyper-masculinized nationalism, circa 1900. In 1896, for example, Adolf Brand founded *Der Eigene* (which could be translated as "The Self Owners"). It was the world's first serious homosexual journal. By the late 1920s, it claimed an astonishing 150,000 subscribers. Critical of a "feminized" male homosexuality, Brand called for a hyper masculinity, complete with man/boy love. As he wrote in a promotional pitch:

> [*Der Eigene* is for men who] thirst for a revival of Greek times and Hellenic standards of beauty after centuries of Christian barbarism.[10]

The journal was also openly racist, nationalistic, and anti-Semitic. In 1902, Brand joined with two known pederasts, Wilhelm Jansen and Benedict Friedlander, to form *Gemeinschaft der Eigenen* ("Community of Self-Owners") to promote homosexual rights, including free access to boys. Friedlander held that heterosexual men, effeminate homosexuals, and women were all inferior beings. Heterosexual love was but a poor necessity, only to be used for procreation. Instead, Friedlander asserted the esthetic superiority of pederast relations. As he wrote in his 1904 book *Renaissance des Eros Uranios* ("Renaissance of Uranian[11] Erotica"):

> The positive goal...is the revival of Hellenic chivalry and its recognition by society. By chivalric love we mean in particular close relationships between youth and even more particularly the bonds between men of unequal ages.

As the "Gay-Lesbian-BiSexual" sourcebook, *We Are Everywhere* (1997), summarizes, the Community of Self-Owners represented "a heady brew of individualism, anarchism, Nietzschean anti-feminism, glorification of pedophilia, and homosexual elitism."[12] In 1920, this Community created the Society for Human Rights, Weimar Germany's leading "homosexual rights" organization, one resting on the same "heady brew."

In 1907, Jorg Lanz von Liebenfels—a former Cistercian monk expelled from this Catholic monastic order for "carnal and worldly desires" [common euphemisms for homosexual acts]—raised the first swastika flag. It flew over the castle which housed his *Ordo Novi Templi*, the "Order of the New Temple." He chose the swastika for its association with the ancient Germanic God, Wotan. Lanz claimed to have restored the old Knights Templar, emphasizing the occult and strange sexual rituals where "perfection is gained by satisfying all of one's desires." His journal, *Ostara*, was named for Wotan's female counterpart. Lanz despised women, writing, "the soul of the woman has something pre-human, something demonic, something enigmatic about it." Articles in *Ostara* carried titles such as "The Dangers of Women's Rights and the Necessity of a Masculine Morality of Masters." As revealed by his own book *Mein Kampf*, young Adolf Hitler was an avid reader of Ostara. Here, he found a racial theory of history proclaiming the holiness of "the one creative race, the Aryans"; a call for a racial elite led by a quasi-religious military leader; a plan for "Aryan" breeding farms; and a proposal [by Lanz] that "unsatisfactory" racial types be eliminated by abortion, sterilization, starvation, and forced labor. All of these ideas would later find fruition in the emergent SS State.[13]

In 1912, advocates of these strange, fantastical, and cruel notions came together to form the Germanen Society. In 1917, its Bavarian chapter became the Thule Society (referring to a supposed northern island refuge of the Lost Race of Atlantis). Thule Society participants included Dietrich Eckart (the founder of the Nazi Party and Hitler's mentor) as well as Rudolf Hess (later Hitler's vice führer). And in 1919, the Nazi Party grew out of The Thule Society: what Samuel Igra calls "a band of evil men who were united together by a common vice."[14]

Recent revisionist historians discount the importance of any early ties between a "common vice" and Nazism, citing later Nazi pronouncements against homosexuality and retention of the Weimar Law making homosexuality a crime. Contemporaries reported otherwise. As Adolf Brand, editor of *Der Eigene*, himself commented in 1930,

> Men such as Captain Röhm…are, to our knowledge, no rarity at all in the National Socialist Party. It rather teems there with homosexuals

of all kinds. And the joy of man in man, which…the Edda [a collection of thirteenth-century mythological poems written in Old Norse] frankly extols…as the highest virtue of the Teutons, blossoms around their campfires and is cultivated and fostered by them in a way done in no other male union that is reared on party politics.[15]

Recent historians also make much of the fact that in May 1933, the Nazis sacked Berlin's Institute for Sex Research and burned thousands of its books and files. The Institute's founder had been Magnus Hirschfield, a non-nationalistic homosexual. These historians say that its destruction underscores the reality of Nazi persecution. In fact, the Institute's assistant director, Ludwig Lenz, has provided another explanation for the action:

> We…had a great many Nazis under treatment at the Institute….We knew too much. It would be against medical principles to provide a list of the Nazi leaders and their perversions [but]…not ten percent of the men who, in 1933, took the fate of Germany into their hands were sexually normal….[W]e possessed about forty thousand confessions and biographical records.[16]

Lively and Abrams do suggest that the confinement and torment of 15,000 homosexuals in the death camps may have had more to do with fabricated accusations and conflicts within the homosexual community than with systematic persecution.[17] However, as I have noted, all this remains a matter of controversy.

In any case, it is safe to conclude that the story about Nazism and homosexuality is far more complicated than we have been led to believe.[18] As Gabriel Jackson, professor of history emeritus at the University of California-San Diego, concludes, "there is simply no historical doubt about the important role of homosexuals and bisexuals in the upper ranks of the Nazi movement from day one to the end."[19] It is also safe to conclude that, surface indications aside, Nazism was no friend of the natural, autonomous family; rather, this movement was one of the family's most vicious foes.

The Communist Family

Communism shared with Nazism a commitment to Left Wing, Darwinian, Evolutionary Socialism. Yet strangely, where this worldview led the Nazis to advocate militant male supremacy over brood females, it led the Communists to embrace full sexual equality.

Friedrich Engels, Karl Marx's friend and collaborator, first developed this argument in his 1884 book, *The Origin of the Family, Private Property and the State*. Appealing to the evolution of the family, Engels called for its end as an economic unit, for elimination of the concept of legitimacy, for the movement of all women into industry, for the collective care and rearing of children, and for easy and unilateral divorce.[20]

Shortly after the Bolsheviks took power in Russia in November, 1917, the Council of Peoples Commissars implemented this "no fault" scheme. Writing a few years later for the journal *Komunistka*, Alexandra Kollontai updated Engel's argument. Notably, she blamed the frailty of the family in the early twentieth century on capitalism:

> There was a time when the isolated, firmly-knit family, based on a church wedding, was equally necessary to all its members.... But over the last hundred years this customary family structure has been falling apart in all the countries where capitalism is dominant.[21]

More forcefully, she emphasized that traditional marriage and family were everywhere headed toward the historical scrapheap, casualties of social-economic evolution:

> There is no escaping the fact: the old type of family has had its day. The family is withering away not because it is being forcibly destroyed by the state, but because the family is ceasing to be a necessity. The state does not need the family, because the domestic economy is no longer profitable.... The members of the family do not need the family either, because the task of bringing up the children which was formerly theirs is passing more and more into the hands of the collective.[22]

Even so, Communists such as Kollontai were not really content to let social evolution or history take its supposed course. Progress needed to be hurried up; backward attitudes eliminated. As another Communist, one Madame Smidovich, explained, "To clear the family out of the accumulated dust of the ages we had to give it a good shakeup; this we did."[23] Some parents, "narrow and petty," failed to see the course of history, and were "only interested in their own offspring." There was no room in communist society for this "proprietary attitude." As Kollontai wrote, "The worker-mother must learn not to differentiate between yours and mine; she must remember that there are only our children, the children of Russia's communist workers." Accordingly, children must be raised by "qualified educators" so that "the child can grow up a conscious communist who recognizes the need for solidarity, comradeship, mutual help and loyalty to the collective." And then:

> In place of the individual and egoistic family, a great universal family of workers will develop, in which all the workers, men and women, will above all be comrades.[24]

Indeed, by 1925, the provision of easy, unilateral divorce—"to be obtained at the [simple] request of either partner in a marriage"—had already undermined many Russian families. As one observer reported in 1926, peasant villages probably suffered the most:

> An epidemic of marriages and divorces broke out in the country districts. Peasants with a respectable married life of forty years and more behind them suddenly decided to leave their wives and remarry. Peasant boys looked upon marriage as an exciting game and changed wives with the change of seasons. It was not an unusual occurrence for a boy of twenty to have had three or four wives, or for a girl of the same age to have had three or four abortions.[25]

In October 1925, the Communists took another step to dismantle the family. The *Tzik*, or Central Executive Committee, considered a bill that would eliminate all distinctions between registered and unregistered marriages, giving a cohabiting woman the same status and property rights as a legal wife. Advocates for the measure stressed that this represented a generous extension of marital benefits. Mr. Kursky, representing the Soviet Commission for Justice, introduced the bill:

> He pointed out that whereas, according to the old law, the wife had no rights in the case of an unregistered marriage, the proposed law would give her the rights of a legal wife in holding property and in other matters. Another new point was that the wife and husband would have an equal right to claim support from the other, if unemployed or incapacitated.[26]

In practice, of course, the bill would have abolished marriage under the ruse of extending marital benefits to new categories of relationships. Strident opposition to the measure, particularly in rural, peasant locales, slowed its full implementation. However, peasant families in The Soviet Union soon faced a much more immediate danger from the Communist authorities.

Opposition to the Bolshevik regime had been rising among the peasantry, who constituted the large majority of the Russian and Ukrainian populations. Many had welcomed the 1917 Revolution as an opportunity to gain clear title to their land, but by 1929 they could see the true aims of the Communists: a destruction of their family-centered way of life. Like small farmers everywhere, the Russian and Ukrainian free peasantry—called Kulaks by the Communists—was composed of large and strong families, involving early and lasting marriages, numerous children, vital home economies, deep attachment to private property and local communities, and a fierce distrust of central authority. In all these ways, they stood athwart the Bolshevik project. During 1929 alone, 1,300 major anti-Soviet riots and mass demonstrations occurred in the countryside; 3,200 Soviet civil servants were victims of so-called "terrorist attacks" in these rural areas. The response, according to the definitive *Black Book of Communism*, was "a war declared by the Soviet state on a nation of small holders;" in essence, a war declared on families.[27]

On December 27, 1929, Party Secretary Josef Stalin ordered "the eradication of all Kulak tendencies and the elimination of the Kulaks as a class." The State Political Directorate, or GPU, organized the campaign. Among families that showed "counter-revolutionary activities," the men were to be executed or put in work camps; their property confiscated; and the women and children deported in cattle cars to Siberia. Even those loyal to the regime were to be forced off their land, and relocated on collectivized farms. Since there was no precise definition of a Kulak, most local Soviet committees used "dekulakization" to settle old scores. "Eat, drink, and be merry for all belongs to us," became the motto of the Dekulakization Brigades.

The violence was terrible. On the family side, during 1930 alone, nearly 2.5 million Russian and Ukrainian peasants took part in

14,000 major revolts, riots, and mass demonstrations, defending their way of life and their liberties. Women, reports say, often took the lead in these protests, particularly when caused by the forced closing of a church. Another 1,500 Soviet civil servants were killed. But the Kulaks had few modern weapons; their guns had been confiscated by the authorities during the prior decade. So in the end, the Soviet Brigades had their way. Over the next two years, tens of thousands of Kulak fathers were directly executed, and two million Kulaks were deported to Siberia. In this great disruption, famine settled over the land and another six million died of starvation. The sight of the dead on village roadsides became routine. Hundreds of thousands more died during the deportations.[28]

The official accounts from the time are eerie, given their bureaucratic tone. This one, though, shows a spark of humanity. It comes from the archives of Novosibirsk:

> On 29 and 30 April…two convoys of 'outdated elements' were sent to us by train…. The first convoy contained 5,070 people, and the second 1,044; 6,114 in all. The transport conditions were appalling: the little food that was available was inedible, and the deportees were cramped into nearly airtight spaces…. The result was a daily mortality rate of 35-40 people. These living conditions, however, proved to be luxurious in comparison to what awaited the deportees on the island of Nazino…. There were no tools, no grain, and no food. That is how their new life began. The day after the arrival of the first convoy, on 19 May, snow began to fall again, and the wind picked up. Starving, emaciated from months of insufficient food, without shelter,…they were trapped…. On the first day, 295 people were buried…. It was not long before the first cases of cannibalism occurred.[29]

Ronald Reagan's famous—and for the time courageous—phrase, "The Evil Empire," actually seems to do insufficient justice to a regime that intentionally committed such acts against families.

Communism has warred against marriage and the family in other places, as well. Communist China, for example, experienced a terrible famine in the 1958-61 period, resulting in a staggering 30 million deaths and another 33 million lost or postponed births: perhaps the greatest politically inspired disaster in human history. The cause? According to two Chinese scholars, simply the suppression of the home-cooked meal.

The target again was marriage and the rural family. Specifically, in August and September of 1958, Communist authorities forced 90 percent of rural Chinese households into huge communes, averaging 23,000 members each. Relative to food the authorities also outlawed family gardens, family orchards, and even family kitchenware. "Private kitchens, as symbols of selfishness, were destroyed," write Gene Hsin Chang and Guanzhong James Wen. The woks and the pots were melted; the law forbade mothers and grandmothers from cooking. All must eat in communal halls.

The results were depressingly familiar. In the dining halls, the members of the commune first turned to gluttony. With no limits on consumption, peasants "in 20 days finished almost all the rice they had, rice that should have lasted six months." Within a year, they were reduced to savagery: "[I]n Gansu and Shandong…some people had to eat their dead children's bodies." The famine ended only when the Communists allowed the return of family gardens and home meals.[30]

Family under "The New Totalitarians"

A philosophically related, if physically non-violent, campaign against marriage and family has also been waged by "The New Totalitarians," historian Roland Huntford's label for the Social Democrats of Sweden.[31] This need not have been Sweden's fate. Within the early Swedish labor movement, there were advocates for the natural family. For workers, they sought a "family wage," a living income for the father and husband that would also support a wife and mother and her children at home. Welfare policies would also be built around this breadwinner-homemaker-child-rich home model. This was Swedish Social Democratic policy between 1940 and 1967. Relative to the family, it worked reasonably well.

But egalitarian feminist pressures for change grew during Sweden's so-called "Red Years," 1967-1976.[32] Oddly enough, but with perverse wisdom, these social radicals turned their first attention to tax policy. The feminist writer Eva Moberg complained that the current tax system, resting on the joint return for married couples and the principle of "income splitting," condemned educated women to "lifetime imprisonment within the four walls of the home." Mathematician Sonja Lyttkens argued that the Swedish tax code had "a large discouraging impact on married women's labor supply."[33] In 1968, a joint report by the Social Democratic Party and the trade union alliance (the LO) concluded that "there are...strong reasons for making the two breadwinner family the norm in planning long-term changes within the social insurance system."[34] The next year, the Social Democratic Party issued its "Report on Equality," prepared by a panel chaired by the feminist Alva Myrdal. The document concluded that "[i]n the society of the future,...the point of departure must be that every adult is responsible for his/her own support. Benefits previously inherent in married status should be eliminated." As part of this legal deconstruction of marriage, the Report called for a tax-policy that abolished the joint return, taxing instead individual earnings without preference for any so-called "form of cohabitation."[35]

Analysts of modern Sweden are virtually unanimous in labeling this 1971 shift from "joint" to "individual" taxation as the most important policy change affecting Swedish social life during the last 40 years. Sven Steinmo calls it "the most significant" and "radical" reform of the turbulent 1970s, because "it meant that the Swedish tax system would ignore family circumstances."[36] Through this change, reports Anne Lise Ellingsaeter, the traditional male provider norm was "more or less eradicated."[37] The influential feminist author Annika Baude adds: "If I were to choose one reform which has perhaps done the most to promote equality between the sexes [in Sweden], I would point to the introduction of individual income taxation."[38] Using a different interpretive lens, it is fair to conclude that Sweden's current regime of few and weak marriages, fragile homes, widespread cohabitation, extensive day care, a retreat from children, and universal employment of young mothers derives—to a significant degree—from this one change in tax policy.

Marriage and Liberty

All these stories, from the terrible and violent campaigns against marriage mounted by the Nazis and the Communists to the quiet assault on marriage launched by Sweden's "Red" Social Democrats, reveal a common truth. The first target of any totalitarian regime is marriage. Why? The great English journalist G. K. Chesterton explains the reason in his provocative 1920 pamphlet, *The Superstition of Divorce*:

> The ideal for which [marriage] stands in the state is liberty. It stands for liberty for the very simple reason...[that] it is the only...institution that is at once necessary and voluntary. It is the only check on the state that is bound to renew itself as eternally as the state, and more naturally than the state.... This is the only way in which truth can ever find refuge from public persecution, and the good man survive the bad government.[39]

Or, as Chesterton explained in his 1910 book, *What's Wrong with the World*:

> It may be said that this institution of the home is the one anarchist institution. That is to say, it is older than law, and stands outside the State.... The State has no tool delicate enough to deracinate the rooted habits and tangled affections of the family; the two sexes, whether happy or unhappy, are glued together too tightly for us to get the blade of a legal penknife in between them. The man and the woman are one flesh—yes, even when they are not one spirit. Man is a quadruped.[40]

And that truth still exhibits itself in our time. For example, the *Polish Sociological Review* carried a recent article on developments in Uzbekistan during the period of Soviet Communist rule. The author writes,

> [O]nly traditional relationships enabled the people to survive the particularly difficult conditions which prevailed throughout the Soviet period....[W]hile the sovietization of Central Asian society rocked the religious and cultural foundations of the family, its basic...features were preserved.

In many cases, the task of preservation fell to women. The author again: "I know of families where the father was a teacher of scientific atheism, while the wife said her prayers five times a day and observed 'ramadan,' so as to (as she put it) atone for her husband's sins." When the Communists fell, and Uzbekistan regained its freedom, these traditions were still there, so that husbands, wives, and their children could rebuild a nation.[41]

A second example comes from The People's Republic of China. As noted earlier, the Chinese peasantry—collectivized on industrial farms by Mao Tse Tung—suffered terribly for nearly two decades, as the Communists sought to eliminate families as "fundamental habitation and production units." But Mao's death in 1976 brought a shift in policy, leading two years later to the introduction of the so-called "family responsibility system." The collective farms were broken up, and families gained the use of land according to their size. After meeting a quota, farm produce was theirs to consume or sell. The new system also allowed peasant families to engage in side occupations.

Results between 1978 and 1990 were spectacular. Farm output climbed sharply, as did rural family wealth and well being. More importantly, traditional marriage patterns reappeared after decades of suppression, as did a preference for many children. In the more rural parts of China, three-quarters of women now wanted four-or-more children. Indeed, this "family responsibility system" subverted in the countryside the post-Mao leadership's other innovation: namely, the "one child per family" population policy.[42]

Dutch scholars, moreover, have documented that the imposition of Communism on Poland after 1945 did not weaken the family system there. Instead, the oppressive Communist system actually increased family solidarity:

> We [found] that the importance of the family increased, and that—as in Hungary after World War II,…the family increased its role as the cornerstone of society. Political and social suppression can have unexpected positive effects, like the strengthening of the family.[43]

As Chesterton had predicted, the natural family—"the one anarchist institution"—survived, and even triumphed over totalitarian Communism, one of its great twentieth-century foes.

Oddly enough, the family's greater challenge may be the "soft" totalitarianism of the early twenty-first century, now packaged around a militant secular individualism, but still seeking to build a marriage-free, post-family order. The immediate targets in this campaign remain the complementarity of the sexes and the autonomy of the home. As with the Nazis and the Communists, the larger goal is still the destruction of the natural family, leaving lone individuals in thrall to the ideological state. The greater power of this campaign derives from its subtlety, its use of the therapeutic to gain the same ends once pursued through open violence.

All the same, I have faith that this effort, too, will fail. For like all other totalitarianisms, it denies vital traits of human nature, traits that win out in the end. Persecution, disaster, even the fall of nations and civilizations cannot destroy the familial character of humankind. "In the break-up of the modern world," Chesterton observed, "the family will stand out stark and strong as it did before the beginning of history; the only thing that can really remain a loyalty, because it is also a liberty."[44]

Notes

1. Claudia Koonz, *Mothers in the Fatherland: Women, the Family, and Nazi Politics* (New York: St. Martin's Press, 1987): xxi-xxxiii.
2. Koonz, *Mothers in the Fatherland*, pp. 14, 393.
3. *Ibid.*, p. 408.
4. *Ibid.*, p. 393.
5. *Ibid.*, p. 398. Emphasis added.
6. *Ibid.*, p. 399. Emphasis added.
7. As examples of this interpretation, see: Richard Plant, *The Pink Triangle: The Nazi War Against Homosexuals* (New York: Henry Holt, 1986); and Gunter Grau, ed., *Hidden Holocaust: Gay and Lesbian Persecution in Germany 1933-45* (London: Cassell, 1995).
8. Samuel Igra, *Germany's National Vice* (London: Quality Press, 1945).
9. Scott Lively and Kevin Abrams, *The Pink Swastika: Homosexuality in the Nazi Party* (Keizer, OR: Founders Publishing Corp., 1995): vii.
10. Quoted in Lively and Abrams, *The Pink Swastika,* pp. 19-22. For a collection of essays from *Der Eigene* in English translation, see: Harry Oosterhuis, *Homosexuality and Male-Bonding in Pre-Nazi Germany* (New York: Harrington Park Press, 1991).
11. Uranian was an early term for homosexual introduced by Karl Ulrichs in 1860: Karl Heinrich Ulrichs, *The Riddle of 'Man-Manly' Love,* trans. Michael A. Lombardi-Nash (New York: Prometheus Books, [1860] 1994): 129-78.
12. Mark Blasins and Shane Phelan, *We Are Everywhere: A Historical Sourcebook of Gay and Lesbian Politics* (New York: Routledge, 1997): 134.
13. See: Nicholas Goodrick-Clarke, *The Occult Roots of Nazism: Secret Aryan Cults and Their Influence on Nazi Ideology* (New York: New York University Press, 1992).

14. Lively and Abrams, *The Pink Swastika*, p. 101.

15. Adolf Brand, "Political Criminals: A Word About the Röhm Case [1931]," in Oosterhuis, *Homosexuality and Male-Bonding in Pre-Nazi Germany*, p. 236.

16. Quotation found at: "International Committee for Holocaust Truth: 1996, Report #3," at: *http://www.e-z.nlt/wtv/v-icht-3.htm* (6/13/2004). Emphasis added. See: Ludwig Lenz, *Memoirs of a Sexologist: Discretions and Indiscretions* (New York: Cadillac Publ. Co., 1951).

17. Lively and Abrams, *The Pink Swastika*, pp. 123-42.

18. For example, the exhibit on the Nazi persecution of homosexuals mounted by the U.S. Holocaust Memorial Museum in 2002-03 ignored homosexuality within the Nazi party, despite the protests of eminent historians.

19. Quoted in Nathaniel Lehrman, "Victims, But No Gay Villains, in Holocaust Museum Exhibit," *Insight* (Feb. 3-17, 2003).

20. Friedrich Engels, *The Origin of the Family, Private Property and the State* (Chicago: Charles H. Kerr & Co., 1902 [1884]).

21. Alexandra Kollontai, "Communism and the Family," Komunistka (No. 2, 1920): 2; at: *http: www.marxists.org/archive/kollonti/works/1920/ communism-family.htm* (6/2/2004).

22. Kollontai, "Communism and the Family," p. 9.

23. A Woman Resident in Russia, "The Russian Effort to Abolish Marriage," Atlantic (July 1926), p. 1; at *http:www.theatlantic.com/cgi-bin/ send.cgi?page=http%3A//www.theatlantic.com/issues/2* (6/2/2004).

24. Kollontai, "Communism and the Family." Pp. 8, 10.

25. A Woman, "The Russian Effort to Abolish Marriage," p. 2.

26. Ibid., p. 3.

27. Stephane Courtois, et al., *The Black Book of Communism: Crimes, Terror, Repression* (Cambridge, MA: Harvard University Press, 1999): 146.

28. Courtois, *The Black Book of Communism*, pp. 146-49.

29. *Ibid.*, p. 154.

30. Gene Hsin Chang and Guanzhong James Wen, "Communal Dining and the Chinese Famine of 1958-1961," *Economic Development and Cultural Change* 46 (October 1997): 1-34.

31. Roland Huntford, *The New Totalitarians* (New York: Stein & Day, 1972).

32. A phrase used by: Yvonne Hirdman, "The Importance of Gender in the Swedish Labor Movement, Or: A Swedish Dilemma," Paper prepared for The Swedish National Institute of Working Life, 2002, p. 5.

33. Siv Gustafson, "Separate Taxation and Married Women's Labor Supply: A Comparison of West Germany and Sweden," *Journal of Population Economics* 5 (1992): 63-64.

34. From: Jane Lewis and Gertrude Åström, "Equality, Difference, and State Welfare: Labor Market and Family Policies in Sweden," *Feminist Studies* 18 (Spring 1992): 67.

35. Alva Myrdal, et. al., *Toward Equality: The Alva Myrdal Report to the Swedish Social Democratic Party* (Stockholm: Prisma; 1972 [1969]): 17, 38, 64, 82-84. See also: Hilda Scott, Sweden's 'Right to Be Human': Sex-Role Equality: The Goal and the Reality (Armonk, NY: M.E. Sharpe, 1982): 3-7.

36. Sven Steinmo, "Social Democracy vs. Socialism: Goal Adaptation in Social Democratic Sweden," *Politics & Society* 16 (Dec. 1988): 430.

37. Anne Lise Ellingsaeter, "Dual Breadwinner Societies: Provider Models in the Scandinavian Welfare States," *Acta Sociologica* 41 (#1, 1998): 66.

38. Annika Baude, "Public Policy and Changing Family Patterns in Sweden, 1930-1977," in Jean Lipman-Blumen and Jessie Bernard, eds., *Sex Roles and Social Policy: A Complex Social Science Equation* (Beverly Hills, CA: Sage, 1979): 171.

39. G.K. Chesterton, *Collected Works: Volume IV: Family, Society, Politics* (San Francisco: Ignatius Press, 1987): 256. Emphasis added.

40. Chesterton, *Collected Works*, IV, pp. 67-68. Emphasis added.

41. Marfua Toktakhodjaeva, "Society and Family in Uzbekistan," *Polish Sociological Review* 2 (1997): 149-165.

42. See: Li Zong, "Agricultural Reform and Its Impact on Chinese Rural Families, 1978-1989," *Journal of Comparative Family Studies* 24 (Autumn 1993).

43. H. Ruigrok, J. Dronkers, B. Mach, "Communism and the Decline of the Family: Resemblance between the occupational levels of Polish siblings from different gender, generations, political background and family forms." Paper presented at the Seventh Social Science Study Day conference, April 11-12, 1996, The University of Amsterdam.

44. *Illustrated London News*, June 17, 1933.

5

"Conjugal Happiness" and the American Style: The Special Relationship between Marriage and the American Experience

The current national crisis over the meaning of marriage is something more than another public debate. The issue of marriage cuts to the very heart of the American identity, to our self-definition as a people.

Some may be surprised to hear this. After all, is not America really a nation of individuals and individualism, of lifestyle experimentation, of moral innovation, with family matters of secondary and fading public importance? Or as contemporary voices ask, does not American democracy stand for the steady expansion of individual rights—including "the right to marry"—to ever more categories of people? As Nathan Glazer explains in his recent book, *We Are All Multiculturalists Now*: "If progress is the spread of equality and liberty, one does not see how any good arguments can be made against gay and lesbian claims."[1]

This is, I believe, a false reading of American history and identity. For alongside affirmation of the integrity and worth of the individual, the American nation has also been a land uniquely defined, from its origin to the modern era, by its commitment to marriage, understood as the bond of man and woman for procreation and the rearing of their children. This defining trait of American nationhood goes well back into colonial times.

Puritan Love

The Puritans, for example, were not the prudish, loveless folk so often parodied in our day. Rather, as Edmund Morgan's classic work, *The Puritan Family*, explains, these early Americans saw

Christian marriage as the foundation of their community. This Puritan vision of love "proceeded from Christian charity," rested on reason and a consciousness of God's sacred order, and was still "warm and tender and gracious."

It is true that a Puritan marriage often began with rational, deliberate choices. Diaries from the time tell of young men setting out to find "a Woman of Merit—a woman of Good Temper and prudent Conduct and Conversation," someone who might be "a meet yoke fellow." All the same, true passion also occupied the Puritan mind. John Winthrop's letters to his wife Margaret commonly ended with phrases such as "I kiss and love thee with the kindest affection" and "with the sweetest kisses and pure embracings of my kindest affection I rest Thine."[2] Among the Puritan's favorite theologians was Thomas Hooker, who compared the relation of husband and wife to that of Christ and the believer, and who called the ordinances of the Church "but the Lord's love letters." Regarding the husband, Hooker wrote of him as a woman's true soulmate:

> The man whose heart is endeared to the woman he loves, he dreams of her in the night, hath her in his eye…when he awakes, museth on her as he sits at table, walks with her when he travels and parties with her in each place where he comes…. She lies in his Bosom, and his heart trusts in her, which forceth all to confess, that the stream of his affection, like a mighty current, runs with full Tide and strength.

Another favorite Puritan theologian, John Cotton, in a commentary on the Canticles, compared the worship of God in church to the marital love of husband and wife:

> [The word delights] is an allusion to the marriage bed, which is the delights of the Bridegroom, and Bride. This marriage-bed is the publick worship of God in the Congregation of the Church (as Can. 3.1).[3]

Alongside such emotional richness, Puritan marriages were also vital in the New World, where the respective skills of husband and wife—their common home economy—were necessary to survival in the agricultural settlements of the Massachusetts Bay Colony.

Backcountry Bonds

The same focus on fruitful marriage could be found among the early backcountry Americans: known in our time as the hillbillies.

During the eighteenth century, tens of thousands of Scots and Ulstermen left the British Isles to settle on the American frontier, particularly in the hill country of the Carolinas and Virginia. Adherents to a strict Calvinism, the Scotch-Irish also carried with them a strong sense of marriage and family. Writes historian Carl Bridenbaugh,

> The conquest of the [American backcountry] was achieved by families....The fundamental social unit, the family, was preserved intact...in a transplanting and reshuffling of European folkways.[4]

Along with Calvinism, these backcountry Scotch-Irish also brought from the old country a distinct set of energetic wedding customs: the mock abduction of brides, often involving ritualized payments of a "body price" and an "honor price;" bidden marriages and bridewain; wild feasts fueled by homemade whiskey, reels, and jigs; the rituals surrounding the wedding chamber; and "the constant presence of Black Betty," representing the sexual side of marriage.

And indeed, these frontier marriages were early and prolific. In the South Carolina Upcountry of the eighteenth century, women married at the average age of nineteen; men at age twenty-one. This early marriage was apparently universal, too. In one Carolina backcountry district with 17,000 white inhabitants, there was not one woman at age twenty-five who was neither wife nor widow. And the families were huge: eight, nine, or ten children per household was the norm. As the Anglican missionary Charles Woodmason reported in the late eighteenth century:

> There's not a cabin but has ten or twelve young people in it...In many cabins you will see ten or fifteen children and grandchildren of one size and the mother looking as young as the daughter.[5]

On the frontier and its independent farms, which was how these Americans lived, marriage and an abundance of children provided security and made good economic sense. Faith, custom, and material realities converged around the wedded estate.

Ben Franklin understood this unique importance of marriage to America. Europe had little surplus land and was filled with crowded urban areas, he noted. Adults commonly avoided marriage until later in life. But in America,

> Land being thus Plenty…and so cheap as that a labouring Man, that understands Husbandry, can in a short Time save Money enough to purchase a Piece of new Land sufficient for a Plantation, whereon he may subsist a Family.

These new farmers were "not afraid to marry" for they could look ahead and see that their children when grown could be provided for as well. Franklin concluded,

> Hence marriages in America are more general, and more generally early, than in Europe.

And such marriages were fertile: eight births to each marriage in America, Franklin estimated, compared to an average of four in old Europe. The true "Fathers of their Nation," Franklin said in reference to the political leaders of his time, would be "The Cause of the Generation of Multitudes, by the Encouragement they afford to Marriage."[6]

Writing in the early 1770s, no less an observer than Adam Smith saw America's culture of marriage as markedly different from that of Europe. The Americans' faith in progress and opportunity, the political economist stressed, found expression through a strong family life:

> The most decisive mark of the prosperity of any country is the increase in its number of inhabitants…. The value of children is the greatest of all encouragements to marriage. We cannot, therefore, wonder that the people in America should generally marry very young.[7]

As historian Barry Shain, looking at the colonial American period, summarizes in his fine book, *The Myth of American Individualism*:

> It appears that…most eighteenth-century Americans cannot be accurately characterized as predominantly individualistic…. The vast majority of Americans lived voluntarily in morally demanding agricultural communities shaped by Reformed Protestant social and moral norms. These communities were defined by overlapping circles of family—and community—assisted self-regulation and even self-denial. [8]

In these family-centered ways, the American colonies differed from Old Europe. Remarkably, the American difference over marriage and marital fertility even transcended the lines of race and slavery. As demographic historian Robert Wells reports in the journal *Population Studies*:

> With regard to marriage and childbearing, black and white women in the South were more like each other than like English women by the second half of the eighteenth century.[9]

Marriage and the New Republic

America's unique bond to marriage continued into the next, or nineteenth century. The good home remained the icon of American self-understanding. The famed French observer of American ways, Alexis de Tocqueville, so testifies. Visiting here in the late 1820s, he found Americans unusually committed to strong and faithful marriages:

> They [Americans] consider marriage as a covenant which is often onerous, but every condition of which the parties are strictly bound to fulfil [sic], because they knew all those conditions beforehand, and were perfectly free not to have contracted them. The very circumstances which render matrimonial fidelity more obligatory, also renders it more easy.

This observation led Tocqueville to a more sweeping conclusion:

> There is certainly no country in the world where the tie of marriage is more respected than in America, or where conjugal happiness is more highly or worthily appreciated…. While the European endeavors to forget his domestic troubles by agitating society, the American derives from his own home that love of order which he afterwards carries with him into public affairs.[10]

Note his words here: Tocqueville held that it was in marriage that Americans crafted the necessary balance between liberty and order. In any democracy, this is the most important of political tasks. Unique in the world, it seems, the nineteenth-century American found the answer in marriage, which transferred an ordered liberty from the home into public life. It is not too much to say that, in Tocqueville's view, the new Republic depended on marriage, rightly understood.

All the same, it is true that in the early years of the nineteenth century, there had been signs that America was losing its sustaining virtues. In 1810, Church membership and attendance were low and falling. Per-capita alcohol consumption soared. So did the proportion of American brides already pregnant when coming to the altar, reaching 30 to 40 percent by 1810.[11]

America's Second Great Awakening, a mass religious revival, came as a response. Tocqueville, we can surmise, caught its spirit. Between 1810 and 1860, there was a dramatic growth in religious participation, particularly among teens and young adults. Formal church membership in America grew explosively, rising 250 percent during these years. In the new climate of religious liberty, dozens of denominations now competed for the allegiance of young members. And while these churches differed in terms of social class and liturgical style, they all affirmed that the regulation of individual morality through marriage and family was a central religious concern.

The results were quite stunning. The proportion of American women who were pregnant at their marriage actually fell from about 35 percent in 1810 to 10 percent by 1850. This was not the result of external laws. Rather, it resulted from a renewed internal sanctity and the exercise of self control; and it underscored that religious and family revival was both possible and a recurring theme of American history. As historians Daniel Scott Smith and Michael Hindus explain, "The sexual revolutionaries of the late eighteenth century, if the premarital procreators may be so labelled, were obviously not the vanguard of a sexually liberated nineteenth century."[12]

Instead, America witnessed the blossoming again of the Christian Home: a new vision captured in the 1869 book, *The American Woman's Home*, co-authored by Catharine Beecher and Harriett Beecher Stowe. These famous sisters described an ideal house church, which would also serve as a home school, with a steeple for a chimney and a movable screen to turn the parlor into a nave. The marital couple also placed an organ in their home for hymn sings and samplers on the walls with favorite Bible verses and Gothic windows pointing toward heaven. As historian Colleen McDannell explains, these homes—Protestant and Catholic alike—rested on pious marriages:

Both the men and women of Victorian America perceived the sacrality of certain household objects. Women might have made or purchased the objects—family Bibles, wax crosses, Angelus clocks—but popular literature often mentioned the objects' emotional impact on men.[13]

And these homes remained strongly committed to children: marital fertility remained high until the end of the nineteenth century, particularly in the South and the Prairie states. Images of the good home, the good marriage, and the primary commitment to children filled the new magazines that characterized the "Victorian Age" in America.

Marriage and American Civilization

As the twentieth century dawned, the importance of marriage to American life found reaffirmation. That great advocate for distinctive American values, Theodore Roosevelt, stressed that in American civilization, marriage was "the most fundamental, the most important of all relations." He continued,

[I]n all the world there is no better and healthier home life, no finer factory of individual character, nothing more representative of what is best and most characteristic in American life, than that which exists in the higher type of family; and this higher type of family is to be found everywhere among us.[14]

For Americans, he wrote,

The primary work of the average man and the average woman—and of all exceptional men and women whose lives are to be really full and happy—must be the great primal work of home-making and home-keeping.[15]

The good marriage, Roosevelt emphasized, would be "a partnership of the soul, the spirit and the mind, no less than of the body." The "highest ideal" of the American family could be achieved "only where the father and mother stand to each other as lovers and friends," and where "the partnership of happiness" would also be "a partnership of work."[16]

This emphasis on marriage and the good home as defining American traits also surfaced as political and cultural leaders faced the challenge of mass immigration in the first two decades of the twentieth century. Over a million new immigrants arrived each year. Compared to the existing population, this was almost three times the flow recorded in the 1990s. Most of these newcomers did not speak English, nor did they practice the Protestant faith, which had been the American norms. How could they be assimilated into American life?

The answer, leading advocates concluded, was through a shared devotion to marriage and family. The common denominator of American identity would be found in building the married-couple home, with husband/fathers seen as "breadwinners" and "home-builders" and wives/mothers seen as "homemakers." As Frances Kellor, director of Americanization Work for the Federal Bureau of Education, explained in 1918,

> If we start with [marriage and] the family and work upward we get a sound city that will stand the strain of any crisis because its weakest links are strong. Every great strain and burden eventually rests upon the family.... Approached from the neighborhood and family and met squarely, the problem of Americanization can be solved adequately.[17]

This work took concrete form in the "Little Mothers Leagues" and the "Baby Saving" campaign organized by the U.S. Children's Bureau in immigrant communities and through the "home economics" teachers funded by the Federal Smith-Lever Act of 1917.

However, these "American values" centered on marriage, home, and family once again showed signs of discord during the 1920s. A rebellion against supposed "repressive" sexual values set in. Religion seemed to be losing its influences on American family life, symbolized by the ridicule heaped on the evangelical lawyer and politician William Jennings Bryan during the Scopes Trial. The "flapper" captured the youthful rebellion against supposed domestic constraints: short skirts; short hair; cigarettes; no marriage; no children. Indeed, the marriage rate tumbled to an historic American low. The total fertility rate among Americans fell from an average of nearly 4 children born per woman in 1890 to only 2 by 1933, for the first time in American history a figure at just the generation replacement rate.

Marriage- and Baby-Booms

However, something extraordinary began to happen in the 1930s. In these years just before World War II, American marriage and fertility rates started to rise. Church membership rolls also began climbing again; indeed, by 1950, nearly half of Americans were attending church or synagogue on any given weekend, a significant increase over the 1930 figure. Moreover, the Protestant churches began once more to show a familistic spirit. Back in 1931, the Federal Council of Churches—representing the so-called Protestant mainline—had broken faith with over a thousand years of Christian consensus and had endorsed family limitation through birth control. In 1946, though, the FCC argued instead that "[f]or the individual family, there is nothing more satisfying, even though it may involve real sacrifice, than to have at least three or four children."[18]

Evangelicals re-entered the public square in these years. In 1949, the young preacher Billy Graham launched a three-week crusade in Los Angeles. With the huge tent overflowing every night, the event extended to nine weeks, and captured national attention.

The American marriage rate soared between 1933 and 1968, recreating a culture of marriage. Just as during the eighteenth century, marriage came early and became nearly universal. And, just as in the nineteenth century, a "liberated" sexuality was reigned in by religiously motivated self-control and by the married state. The average age for first marriage fell to twenty for women and twenty-two for men, very close to the astonishing numbers found among the Carolina backwoodsmen of 1750.

This chart below shows the mid-century American "marriage boom," from a low in 1932, which is used as the base here, to a peak in the late 1940s, showing strength as late as 1970, finally disappearing only in the 1980s. By the early 1960s, over 95 percent of American women had married before age 40. And the American birthrate climbed, too: from a total fertility rate of two children per woman in 1933 to 3.8 in 1957, an increase of 90 percent in less than twenty-five years. Protestant Sunday schools were swarming with children again, and the greatest era of new church construction in American history commenced out in the child-rich suburbs.

The Mid-Century "Marriage Boom"

Year	Marriage Rate*	% Above Base Year of 1932
1932	56.0	0%
1936	74.0	+ 32%
1940	82.8	+ 48%
1944	76.5	+37%
1948	98.5	+ 76%
1952	83.2	+49%
1956	82.4	+47%
1960	73.5	+31%
1964	74.6	+33%
1968	79.1	+41%
1970	76.5	+37%
1976	65.2	+16%
1982	61.4	+10%
1986	56.2	+ 1%
1990	54.5	- 3%
1996	49.7	- 9%

*Marriages per 1,000 Unmarried Women, fifteen years and older

The deeper revolution, though, may have been among American Catholics. Indeed, one might actually see the American "Marriage Boom" and the more famous "Baby Boom" as, statistically speaking, primarily "Catholic things." For example, in a survey conducted during the early 1950s, only 10 percent of Catholics under age forty had four or more children, very close to the 9 percent found among Protestants. By the late 1950s—a mere six years later—the Protestant figure was still 9 percent, but the number of large Catholic families had more than doubled, to 22 percent.[19]

More surprisingly, this surge in Catholic family creation in married-couple homes was most pronounced among Catholic women who had attended college, a development confounding a supposed law of sociology. The commitment to large families was also concentrated among younger believers. Through 1965, each new age cohort of young Catholics was more pro-natalist than the group before. In addition, more frequent attendance at Mass was related to early marriage and high fertility.

Why did this happen? Part of the answer lies, I believe, with a then-unified Teaching Church which—from the Pope on down—focused on the holiness of family creation. As Pope Pius XII told an audience in 1958, "Large families are most blessed by God and specially loved and prized by the church as its most precious treasures."[20] Part of the answer also lies with the new opportunities for early marriage and family creation that came as young Catholics poured out of urban ethnic ghettoes for the new homes on spacious lots in the burgeoning suburbs: a process that Benjamin Franklin had himself anticipated 200 years before.

In sum, religious renewal, and America's abundance of opportunity proved to be a powerful and successful combination, together renewing the Nation. Ordered liberty, resting on marriage, had found new expression.

Economic historian, and later National Security Advisor, Walt W. Rostow underscored the importance of this social renewal to American foreign policy, in his 1957 essay, "The American Style." The nation now confronted the world historical task of facing down Communism, an immense challenge. And yet, Rostow drew hope from "the birth rate increase" witnessed since the 1930s. Compared to old Europe, the America style also included "a narrower but perhaps more intense family," "earlier marriages,…more children," and strong churches and voluntary associations, which worked "to ramify and to weave a highly individualistic and mobile population into a firm social fabric."[21] Much like Tocqueville, Rostow saw this nation's commitment to marriage and family as vital to the success of American democracy. As he wrote in the official U.S. "Basic National Security Policy" report for 1962,

> The success of the whole [anti-communist] doctrine and strategy developed in this paper depends on the capacity of the U.S. to sustain a performance at home which reaches deeply into our domestic arrangements and which requires widespread…assumption of responsibility and sacrifice for public purposes by our people.[22]

Without such grounding in a nation of decent and child-centered homes, Rostow believed, American national security policy would stumble and fail; and so it happened in the decade after 1965.

Family Wars

Indeed, starting in that portentous year, a culture-wide attack on the institution of marriage began. Neo-Malthusians seeking population control; feminists seeking a "liberation" from traditional home life; sexual revolutionaries striving to tear down religious guides and restraints; and socialists seeking to eliminate all institutions standing between the individual and the state: all shared an interest in destroying this latest iteration of America's unique culture of marriage. Between 1965 and 1980, they largely had their way. As the Playboy Press, in its "Official History of the Sex Revolution," boasted as early as 1973,

> Legions of Lolitas joined the battle [against American values].... Manners and morals and great institutions bit the dust.... And when the air was cleared...the world was never going to be the same again. No one knew exactly how, but Western Civilization had been caught with its pants down.

Appropriately, this book's lead title was *Rape of the A*P*E**, APE here meaning the American Puritan Ethic. A subtitle—*The Obscening of America*—underscored the intentional nature of the enterprise, led by men "dirty-minded beyond belief." The Playboy Press concluded that this revolution had "removed America's backbone" and had revealed our nation's terrible secret:

> Stripped of the Puritan ethic, we have no morals at all.... [N]othing was reduced to less recognizable rubble than the revered Institution of Marriage.[23]

So sayeth the Playboy Press.

Well, if Benjamin Franklin, Adam Smith, Alexis de Tocqueville, and Theodore Roosevelt were all correct regarding the special place of marriage in the building of the American Republic, then the Playboy Press is equally correct in underscoring how the assault on traditional marriage launched in the 1960s and 1970s was also an assault on the very foundation of our Republic: "the revered Institution of Marriage." The changes might be summarized through the following numbers, comparing 1957—the height of the mid-twentieth century "Marriage Boom"—to the year 2000:

	1957	2000
Marriage Rate (a)	82.4	47.2
Percentage of Adult Males Married	76.6	61.5
Median Age at First Marriage (for women)	20.3	26.0
Married Couple Households, as a % of All Households	76%	53%
Marital Fertility Rate (b)	161.4	92.9

a = Marriages per 1000 unmarried women, ages 15 and older
b = Births per 1000 married women, ages 18 to 44.

Here we see a sharp decline in the marriage rate (by about 43 percent), a retreat from marriage among both men and women, the near disappearance of early marriage, the weakening of the married-couple home as the normative American lifestyle, and a sharp fall in what one analyst calls "the marital product"—that is, children. And not by coincidence, these were also the years of American retreat from the world symbolized by the fall of Saigon to Communism and the Iranian hostage crisis.

Cultures of Marriage

However, despite claims of victory by the sexual left, and despite even recent scenes from Massachusetts, a "culture of marriage" still survives in America. We can, for example, find it among certain religious groups. The Southern Baptist Convention (SBC), as example, is the largest Protestant body in America, with 16 million members. Its 1998 resolution on "the family" scandalized progressive opinion. The SBC measure stated that "God has ordained the family as the foundational institution of human society"; that "Marriage is the uniting of one man and one woman in covenant commitment for a lifetime"; and, more controversially, that:

> A husband is to love his wife as Christ loved the church. He has the God-given responsibility to provide for, to protect and to lead his family. A wife is to submit herself graciously to the servant leadership of her husband even as the church willingly submits to the headship of Christ. She…has the God-given responsibility to respect her husband and to serve as his helper in managing the household and nurturing the next generation.

Recent data also shows that conservative Protestants who attend church weekly have stronger marriages and more children than the national average. Some have even suggested that we may be on the cusp of, or already engaged in, another Great Awakening, where America's reservoir of religious belief might refresh our culture again.

Meanwhile, another religious group, The Church of Jesus Christ of Latter-day Saints—or The Mormons—has also shown a strong defiance of the spirit of the age and has nourished its own culture of marriage. LDS leaders issued their Proclamation on the Family in 1995, declaring that:

> The first commandment that God gave to Adam and Eve pertained to their potential parenthood as husband and wife. We declare that God's commandment for his children to multiply and replenish the earth remains in force....
>
> The family is ordained of God. Marriage between man and woman is essential to His eternal plan. Children are entitled to birth within the bonds of matrimony, and to be reared by a father and a mother who honor marital vows with complete fidelity.

Brigham Young University, now the nation's largest independent institution of higher learning, expresses this spirit. Expectations of early marriage and family creation are part of the campus atmosphere, physically expressed by the statuary on the campus grounds that features positive images of motherhood, fatherhood, children, and home. In Utah, where LDS members constitute about 70 percent of the population, marital fertility rose between 1987 and 2000, to a figure nearly 50 percent above the U.S. average.

And America's culture of marriage survives in another, most unexpected place: Hollywood. What do the following films have in common?

> *Sleepless in Seattle*
> *Pretty Woman*
> *Runaway Bride*
> *You've Got Mail*
> *Kate and Leopold*
> *Sweet Home Alabama*
> *Maid in Manhattan*
> *Notting Hill*
> *My Big Fat Greek Wedding*
> *Thirteen Going on Thirty*

My daughters call such films "chick flicks." But a better label might be "marriage flicks," for all of them cast marriage as the great, satisfying, and truly fulfilling event in a woman's life, and in a man's life as well. None of these films, let alone the whole genre, could have been made in cynical, libertine, post-marriage Old Europe. Twenty-first century Europeans do not believe in Cinderella anymore; Americans still do, despite the battering that marriage has taken in recent decades. These films are distinctly American: signs of a still-extant cultural yearning for marriage and home.

I tell this story to underscore the profoundly radical and destructive nature of the assault on marriage, now mounted under the labels, "freedom to marry" and "gay rights." These movements are not attempts to fulfill the promise of America. Rather, they seek to undermine the very self-understanding of this nation, our identity as a people. For traditional, natural marriage forms the true American way. As Tocqueville found, marriage is necessary to, or the source of the unique balance between liberty and order that has defined and sustained our Republic. It is a critical part of our unwritten constitution. To tinker with marriage for ideological ends is to place the nation's political order at grave risk.

And I also underscore my belief that America may have the religious and cultural reserves necessary to restore a culture of marriage, provided that public policy once again affirms and supports this traditional institution. Our history offers earlier examples of renewal: the first half of the nineteenth century; and the middle decades of the twentieth century. A third Awakening could emerge in the new century as well, if the nation's political leaders lay the necessary foundation.

Notes

1.   Nathan Glazer, *We Are All Multiculturalists Now* (Cambridge, MA: Harvard University Press, 1997): 18.
2.   Edmund S. Morgan, *The Puritan Family: Religion and Domestic Relations in Seventeenth-Century New England* (New York: Harper and Row, 1966 [1944]): 54-60.
3.   In Morgan, *The Puritan Family*, pp. 60-64, 164.
4.   Quoted in David Hackett Fisher, *Albion's Seed*, found at: *http://xroads. virginia.edu/~UG97/albion/amariag.html; afertili.html*; and *aclan. html*.

5. Quoted in Fisher, *Albion's Seed*, afertili.html.
6. Benjamin Franklin, "Observations Concerning the Increase of Mankind," in Leonard W. Labaree, ed., *The Papers of Benjamin Franklin, Vol. 4* (New Haven, CT: Yale University Press, 1961): 225-34.
7. Adam Smith, *The Wealth of Nations* [1776]: Book 1, Chapter 8, "Of the Wages of Labour," at http://geolib.com/smith.adam/won1:-08.html.
8. Barry Alan Shain, *The Myth of American Individualism* (Princeton, NJ: Princeton University Press, 1994): vi.
9. Robert W. Wells, "The Population of England's Colonies in America: Old English or New Americans?" *Population Studies* 46 (1992): 95.
10. Alexis de Tocqueville, *Democracy in America, Book Three*, Chapter XI; at: http.marxists.org/reference/archive/de-tocqueville/democracy-america/ch35.htm
11. Robert V. Wells, "Family Size and Fertility Control in Eighteenth Century America: A Study of Quaker Families," *Population Studies* 25 (1971): 80-82.
12. Daniel Scott Smith and Michael S. Hindus, "Premarital Pregnancy in America, 1640-1971: An Overview and Interpretation," *Journal of Interdisciplinary History* 5 (1975): 537-39, 551-53.
13. Colleen McDannell, *The Christian Home in Victorian America*, 1840-1900 (Bloomington: Indiana University Press, 1986): xiii-xvii, 1-14, 16, 151-54.
14. Theodore Roosevelt, "The Man Who Works With His Hands," address at the Semi Centennial Celebration of the Founding of Agriculture Colleges in the United States, Lansing, Michigan, May 31, 1907, in *The Works of Theodore Roosevelt: Memorial Edition,* Vol. XVIII (New York: Charles Scribner's Sons, 1924): 188. Emphasis added.
15. Roosevelt, *Works, XVIII*: 228.
16. John A. Lester, ed., *The Americanism of Theodore Roosevelt* (Boston: Houghton Mifflin, 1923): 69.
17. Frances A. Kellor, *Neighborhood Americanization: A Discussion of the Alien in a New Country and of the Native American in His Home Country.* An address to the Colony Club in New York City, Feb. 8, 1918; Wisconsin State Historical Society Pamphlet Collection (Madison), #54-997.
18. In C. Gregg Singer, *The Unholy Alliance* (New Rochelle, NY: Arlington House, 1975): 179.
19. William D. Mosher, David P. Johnson, and Marjorie C. Horn, "Religion and Fertility in the United States: The Importance of Marriage Patterns and Hispanic Origin, " *Demography* 23 (Aug. 1986): 367-69.
20. Pius XII, "The Large Family Address to The Association of Large Families of Rome and Italy, Jan. 19, 1958," *The Pope Speaks* 4 (Spring 1958): 363-64.

21. Walt W. Rostow, "The National Style," in Elting E. Morison, ed., *The American Style: Essays in Value and Performance* (New York: Harper & Brothers, 1958): 246-313.

22. S/P Draft, "Basic National Security Policy," March 26, 1962, Lyndon B. Johnson Papers, Vice-Presidential National Security File, Box 7, Lyndon B. Johnson Library, Austin, TX.

23. Allen Sherman, *The Rape of the A*P*E*: The Official History of the Sex Revolution. The Obscening of America* (Chicago: The Playboy Press, 1973).

6

The Necessity of Marriage Policy

What are the proper ends, or purposes of government? One intelligent answer came from the British author, C.S. Lewis, who wrote,

> It is easy to think the State has a lot of different objects—military, political, economic, and what not. But in a way things are much simpler than that. The State exists simply to promote and to protect the ordinary happiness of human beings in this life. A husband and wife chatting over a fire, a couple of friends having a game of darts in a pub, a man reading a book in his own room or digging in his own garden—that is what the State is there for. And unless they are helping to increase and prolong and protect such moments, all the laws, parliaments, armies, courts, police, economics, etc., are simply a waste of time.[1]

The source of this reflection is Lewis' Christian apologetic, *Mere Christianity*. There is a special charm in Lewis' view of government as being in service to the husband and wife chatting before a fire, to gardening, to "ordinary happiness." This latter phrase actually should hold a special resonance with Americans; after all, the Declaration of Independence commits this nation to the advancement of certain inalienable rights, notably "life, liberty, and the pursuit of happiness."

What a curious and novel idea: a nation devoted to the pursuit of happiness. What did the Founders have in mind here? In her fine book examining the origin and meaning of this phrase, historian Jan Lewis found that "it was within the family circle that men and women [of Jefferson's Virginia] told each other to look for happiness, and there, if anywhere, that they found it." She added, "Virginians who rhapsodized about the family were creating and

97

reinforcing an article of faith for their society, a belief perhaps more central to their lives than any other."

In short, it appears that for the Founders, happiness meant domestic happiness, the life of marriage and family. In this sense, a purpose of the new American nation was to serve family happiness. Despite this record, however, many Americans are bothered today by public attention to the family, especially by the concepts of "marriage-" and "family policy." Some catch the faint whiff here of a dreaded "theocracy," a veiled attempt to impose religious values on a diverse populace. Others are troubled by the specter of governmental meddling in private life.

In response, I argue in this chapter for "the necessity of marriage policy." I will focus on three questions: Why have marriage and the family emerged as central cultural and political issues? What has been the past nature of marriage policy? And: What are the policy imperatives for America in this new century?

The Centralizing State

Answers lie in our history. In one sense, as both the C.S. Lewis and Jan Lewis books remind us, marriage and the family have always been at the center of Anglo-American political concern. It is true that the U.S. Constitution, unlike the basic laws in many other lands, makes no reference to family relations. Even its language is cast in remarkably "gender-neutral" terms, using words such as "person" where the generic "he" would have been expected. This was not due, however, to a remarkably early outbreak of feminism among the Founders nor to an assumption by them that marriage and the family were irrelevant. Rather, these institutions were deeply rooted in what we might call the unwritten Constitution of these new United States, in the cultural and social assumptions about the social order that must be present to sustain a free republic.

The Founders agreed with the ancient Roman statesman Cicero that the family household was the seedbed of virtue and of the political state. Historians underscore how the colonists had left the Old World, hoping that America would be a better setting in which to raise their true and precious "Tender Plants": that is, according to one Quaker writer, "a good place to train up children amongst sober people and to prevent the corruption of them here by the loose behavior of youths and the bad example of too many of riper years." Historian James Henretta shows how late eighteenth-century Americans raised children to "succeed them," not merely to "succeed." In his provocative book The Myth of American Individualism, Barry Shain shows that the American Revolution had more to do with the defense of "familial independence" than it did with quests for personal liberation.

These Americans saw family households as the source of new citizens, the places where the character traits necessary to free government would be forged, the foundation of ordered liberty. Defense of this society of households lay with the states, local communities, and the people. This stance rested, in turn, on the spirit found in the Bill of Rights, especially in the Ninth and Tenth Amendments which affirmed the rights of the people and the powers of the states as bulwarks against centralized authority.

Since the late nineteenth century, however, the scope of government—state and federal—has grown massively. Relative to the family, there were two important changes. First, the legal doctrine of parens patriae—literally "the parenthood of the state"—spawned early examples of interventionist government in movements such as the "reform school" campaign. Federal programs such as Social Security would also pass Constitutional muster only through appeal to parens patriae. Second, the Fourteenth Amendment to the Constitution became a legal wedge for the steady expansion of federal authority at the expense of the states and local communities, and of the families they sheltered. A detailed list of court cases affecting family life could lead to this conclusion: with only a few exceptions, the legal history of the last 125 years can be written as the slow surrender of the Ninth and Tenth Amendments to the growing sweep of the Fourteenth and to the exercise of parens patriae.

Today, the very size and pervasiveness of the federal government—comprising as it does over 25 percent of Gross Domestic Product and involved in every aspect of American life—mandate attention to marital and family relations in federal policymaking. Whatever our theoretical preferences, the original American plan—leaving such issues to the states, local communities, and the people—is not a real option in the age of the U.S. Department of Education, TANF grants, Social Security, the Department of Homeland Security, and federal child care policy.

The federal tax code, to choose another example, also mandates close attention to family questions. Once a tax of any sort claims more than about 5 percent of income or assets, it ceases to be a mere nuisance and starts to influence behavior. Both the federal income and payroll taxes fall into this category. Important issues arise: Should marriage be treated as an economic partnership? Should the unit of taxation be the household? Or the individual? Should children be treated as a consumption choice? Or should the appearance and nurture of children enjoy recognition and special treatment? Should taxation treat "human capital" the same as "physical capital"? Should parenthood be recognized? Neutrality here is not possible.

Or consider the U.S. Army. Our standing army of 1895—30,000 strong, mostly scattered in military posts out West—could rely on a largely bachelor enlisted force and avoid issues of wives and children. However, a standing army of 800,000 men and women, complemented by over 200,000 children in Pentagon-run day care centers, cannot avoid family questions.

So, our situation is this: On the one hand, a fundamental truth has not changed. The family household rooted in marriage remains the most reliable source of new citizens able to sustain a regime of ordered liberty. (Indeed, viewed a different way, America's prisons today are dominated by young adults who grew up in unstable homes, commonly without fathers; there's little prospect for ordered liberty here). On the other hand, new historical circumstances demand that the marriage perspective be a vital lens for federal policymaking.

"Modernity" and Social Crisis

More broadly, that tangle of revolutions called "modernity" also mandates policy attention to marriage and the family. Before the industrial revolution, before the rise of great cities, let us remember, virtually the whole of humankind lived in family-centered economies. For hundreds of human generations, the family household was the center of most productive activity. In the United States, circa 1800, the vast majority of the free population were farmers. Most of the remaining citizens were family-scale artisans and shop-keepers also maintaining home gardens, family cows, and flocks of chickens. Marriages represented the union of complementary, productive skills. Each family raised most of its own food, made most of its own clothing, provided most of its own fuel, and crafted most of its own furniture.

"Modernity" tore through this settled way of life. The family household ceased to be the center of productive labor. Centralized factories, warehouses, and offices displaced home workshops, gardens, and storehouses. Cash exchanges pushed aside the altruistic exchanges of the family. Wives, husbands, and children alike were pulled out of their homes into the wage laborer ranks. Family bonds, once the source of economic strength, now stood more as obstructions to the efficient allocation of labor. The individual, unencumbered and alone, was the new ideal worker.

The status of marriage changed. In the pre-industrial order, husbands and wives had specialized in their labor according to their respective strengths and talents, so that their small family enterprises might succeed. Industrial managers, in contrast, preferred the androgynous individual, sexless, interchangeable.

The status of children also changed. In an agrarian and artisan economy, children—even small ones—were economic assets, parts of small family enterprises. Accordingly, fertility on the family farm and in the artisan's shop tended to be high. However, in the new order, children were either pulled away into an early—and sometimes dangerous—economic independence or the children became liabilities, left at home by working parents to fend for themselves. Fertility plummeted, as actual or potential parents avoided taking on these new little burdens. Indeed, two leading analysts of modern fertility decline, Kingsley Davis writing in 1937 and John C. Caldwell writing in 2003, have both concluded that "the family is not indefinitely adaptable to modern society, and this explains the declining birth rate."[7] Indeed, no developed nation today can claim even replacement level fertility. In many lands, ranging from Russia to Italy to Singapore, fertility levels are perilously low; children are disappearing, threatening even national survival.[8]

Models European and American

And so, these common products of urban-industrial "modernity"—weakened marriages and low fertility—are another reason for the contemporary need to build marriage policy. As Davis and Caldwell imply, the family is not an institution capable of drastic change. Rather, it is a set of relationships rooted in human nature: "natural," in the sense of being biologically grounded; and universal, for being found in every healthy human society. It is also the only proven source of citizens suited to ordered liberty. In modernity's wake, the critical tasks became—and remain—the protection of the natural family from certain pressures of "modernity." Specifically, family policy has meant constructing selected barriers around the home, to limit the spread of the industrial principle, to preserve some domain of family autonomy in the modern industrial order.

Early on, somewhat different approaches were tried in Europe and America, although both were tied to a common family ideal that would bring at least the mother and children back home. Starting around 1900, Europeans consciously built family policies that would protect marriage and raise fertility. The first intellectually consistent efforts to lay out a family policy drew inspiration from Pope Leo XIII's 1891 encyclical Rerum Novarum (The New Age). Rejecting the wage theories of both laissez-faire liberalism and socialism, Leo called instead for an economy based on "the natural and primeval right of marriage" and "the society of the household." Any just wage would enable the father "to provide comfortably for himself, his wife, and children." This goal of a "family wage" received more direct affirmation in Pope Pius XI's 1931 encyclical, Quadragesimo Anno (Forty Years After). Pius declared that "[e]very effort must be made" to insure "that fathers of families receive a wage large enough to meet ordinary family needs adequately."

Using these principles, lay political leaders in France, Belgium, and other European lands proceeded to build family policy systems. The favored approach became "family allowances" that would recognize the disproportionate burdens carried by male laborers with wives and children at home. Business leaders began introducing family allowances on a private basis in 1916. The French government passed laws in the early 1920s creating "equalization funds" within industries, which eliminated any incentive employers might have to avoid hiring workers with families. Besides paying generous allowances on a per child basis, these funds also provided families with marriage loans, pre-natal care, midwives, visiting nurses, birth and breastfeeding bonuses, medical care for children, layettes, and fresh milk. During the late 1930s, these quasi-private funds were absorbed into the French government's emerging Social Security program, and placed under state controls.

In America, policy construction to protect families took a somewhat different, and arguably more successful, course. To begin with, the labels "marriage policy" or "family policy" were rarely used in a direct way; "child welfare" was the preferred moniker. Nor were there many open appeals to "pro-natalist" goals. Still, the ideal of a "family wage" also came to govern American policy formation.

Inspired by "Maternalist" reformers such as Julia Lathrop, Josephine Baker, and Florence Kelly, the U.S. Congress created the Children's Bureau in 1912. Lathrop, named the Bureau's first chief, laid out guiding principles for current and future American policy:

> The power to maintain a decent family living standard is the primary essential of child welfare. This means a living wage and wholesome working life for the men, a good and skillful mother at home to keep the house and comfort all within it. Society can afford no less and can afford no exceptions. This is a universal need.

Pursuing the goal of "Baby Saving," the Children's Bureau also set out to reduce infant and maternal mortality and to improve early child care. The Bureau sponsored "Baby Weeks" to promote good mothering. The Smith-Lever Vocational Training Act of 1917 provided Federal funds to school districts to promote education for girls in the "household arts." The Sheppard-Towner Act of 1921, the first true federal entitlement, provided federal funds to the states for pre-natal and child health clinics and visiting nurses for pregnant and post-partum mothers.

The Great Depression of the 1930s was as much a marital, or family, crisis, as one strictly of economics. Both American marriage and fertility rates fell sharply during the early 1930s. The New Deal, constructed in response by the Franklin D. Roosevelt administration, expanded the scope of the "family wage" ideal in federal policymaking. For example, the National Industrial Recovery Act of 1934 codified sex-defined job categories (that is, "men's jobs" and "women's jobs") with large pay differentials favoring men. The Social Security Amendments of 1939 provided homemakers pensions to women married to eligible men and "survivors" benefits to the widows and children of covered male workers. The National Housing Act created the FHA mortgage program featuring long-term amortization, a low down payment, and insurance protection for the lender. Joined in 1944 by the Veterans Administration (VA) mortgage program, billions of new dollars were mobilized for home construction, with 99 percent of these government-backed mortgages targeted on young married couples. Tax reforms in 1944 and 1948 extended the marriage-friendly benefits of "income splitting" to all American couples and substantially raised the real value of the tax deduction for dependent children.[12]

The results, relative to family statistics, were impressive. Between 1935 and 1963, the marriage rate rose by 30 percent, the average age of first marriage fell to historic lows (age twenty-two for men; age twenty for women), the proportion of ever-married adults reached a record high (over 95 percent), and the marital fertility rate—after falling for 100 years—nearly doubled. Following the turmoil of World War II, even the divorce rate declined between 1946 and 1957. While certainly not wholly due to public policy (see chapter 5), it seems true that family policy initiatives crafted between 1912 and 1948 affirmed, encouraged, and partially caused the remarkable "marriage-" and "baby-booms" of mid-twentieth-century America.[13]

The Sixties and Beyond

And yet, starting in the mid-1960s, the "family model" that had undergirded policymaking in both Western Europe and the United States—the breadwinner/ homemaker/child-rich family sustained by a "family wage"—entered into crisis. Critics of this system suddenly dominated public debates. Atheist, neo-Malthusian, humanist, feminist, socialist, Marxist, playboy philosopher: all agreed on common foes, the breadwinner/homemaker marriage and the child-rich home. A joint assault had policy effects. "No fault" divorce statutes weakened the institutional nature of marriage. Civil rights regulations premised on gender equality eliminated the family wage. Population policy refocused on the so-called "population bomb," with calls for dramatic reductions in family size. Day care subsidies grew; "at home" parenting was ignored. Housing policies came to favor so-called "new family forms." Pro-family tax codes disappeared in favor of individualized taxation, spawning marriage penalties and a shift of the federal tax burden onto married-couple homes with children.[14] Welfare systems came to favor out-of-wedlock childbearing and to penalize family inter-generational care.

Not surprisingly, family statistics reversed course. The marriage rate tumbled. The divorce rate soared. Marital fertility fell by 50 percent. Out-of-wedlock births climbed sharply.

In addition to the hostile ideologies noted above, there were in-ternal weaknesses that left vulnerable the restored American family system of the mid-twentieth century. Specifically, the new Suburban Family of the 1950s rested on an assumption of the "companion-ate" model of marriage, which emphasized psychological tasks such as "personality adjustment" and exaggerated gender roles (for example, the role of the "glamour girl" for wives) to the exclusion of true complementarity and meaningful household functions. In addition, homemaking women and adolescents were increasingly isolated in suburban developments without viable central places for the building of healthy community. Breadwinning men, for their part, engaged in long commutes and were too often only occasional figures in their homes.

There were other problems after 1945. With the old Maternal-ists moving into retirement, policy making elites showed confu-sion over America's mid-century marriage policy achievements, leaving them vulnerable. Specifically, when the "family wage" concept came under challenge, few were able or willing to defend it. Moreover, African Americans never fully entered the family model of the 1950s, with the proportion of out-of-wedlock births soaring, a policy failure ably dissected in Daniel P. Moynihan's 1965 report, *The Negro American Family: The Case for National Action*.[15] Finally, certain "internal contradictions" within the Social Security system also emerged, including disincentives to bear children and a hostility to direct intergenerational care.

A New Marriage Policy

What, then, should be done? Marriage- and family policy is needed today: (1) to insure protection of the married-couple family as an institution in the context of the modern centralizing state; (2) to shelter the integrity and the necessary functions of the family from excessive intrusion by "modernity"; and (3), to respond to the "post-family" ideologies that dominated policymaking from the mid-1960s into the 1980s, and that damaged the only institution capable of sustaining "ordered liberty."

It is also true that any coherent attempt at making family policy must rest on a clear definition of "family," against which one can chart progress or retreat, success or failure. One approach comes from a working group of the World Congress of Families, crafted in May, 1998, in a second-century BC room in the ancient city of Rome. Informed both by the ideals of the Universal Declaration of Human Rights and by the findings of social science, it reads,

> The natural family is the fundamental social unit, inscribed in human nature, and centered around the voluntary union of a man and a woman in a lifelong covenant of marriage for the purposes of: satisfying the longings of the human heart to give and receive love; welcoming and ensuring the full physical and emotional development of children; sharing a home that serves as the center for social, educational, economic, and spiritual life; building strong bonds among the generations to pass on a way of life that has transcendent meaning; and extending a hand of compassion to individuals and households whose circumstances fall short of these ideals.

In addition, as implied above, a family policy fit for the twenty-first century should not try to recreate the framework of fifty years before. It must do better. Specifically, a new American "marriage policy" should:

- Embrace all American ethnic groups in the scheme.
- Affirm marriage as a public good and the marital couple as an economic partnership.
- Balance the equality and the complementarity of men and women.
- Bring both mothers and fathers as well as their children home, through the rebuilding of function-rich, vital home economies.
- Value the birth of new children in married couple homes and honor the special gift to society of the large family.
- Expand the child care choices to include indirect support for the care of preschool children in their homes.
- And celebrate the intact home as the best insurance against abuse, neglect, and delinquency.

With these assumptions in place, a progressive "marriage policy" for this new century would include:

- The legal status (and label) of marriage, together with the substantive financial benefits that it confers, should be confined to the monogamous bond of one man to one woman. While true to our civilization's sexual constitution, this principle also recognizes that it is this bond alone which produces the children likely to be fit for a regime of ordered liberty. With marriage recently transformed into a national issue, an amendment of the U.S. Constitution to safeguard the public interest in marriage now seems imperative. Meanwhile, other human relationships and friendships are properly left unregistered, and unregulated.
- Federal and state public welfare programs (including Temporary Assistance to Needy Families [TANF] grants) should be fully reconfigured to reward marriage among aid recipients, and so encourage them along the most effective path to economic independence.
- The states should re-introduce "fault" into their laws governing divorce (when children are involved), to underscore the communal nature of marriage and the responsibility held by the community toward the young.
- All governments should treat marriage as a full economic partnership. At the federal level, this would mean reintroducing full "income splitting" in the income tax, as existed between 1948 and 1963. Such a measure would eliminate the most notorious "marriage penalty."

- The federal government should reconfigure federal population policies to welcome large families, created responsibly through marriage, as special gifts to our society, deserving affirmation and encouragement.
- To encourage the fruits of marriage, the federal government should double the real value of the personal income tax exemption for children (currently $3,200 per child to $6,400) and of the child tax credit (currently $1,000 per child under age 16 to $2,000) and eliminate income-based restrictions on their availability.
- To protect specialization within marriage, the federal government should replace the existing Dependent Care Tax Credit with a universal, indexed tax credit of $2,500 per child, ages birth to five. This credit would be available to all parents of preschoolers, both those with a parent full time at home and those purchasing substitute care.
- And the Social Security system should reward responsible maternity, as well. For each child born, a married mother should receive three years (or twelve quarters) of employment credits (calculated at the median full-time income) toward her future pension.

On these legal foundations, a new culture of marriage might grow again in America.

Notes

1. C.S. Lewis, *Mere Christianity* (New York: Simon & Schuster Touchstone, 1996): 169.
2. Jan Lewis, *The Pursuit of Happiness: Family and Values in Jefferson's Virginia* (Cambridge: Cambridge University Press, 1983): 204-05.
3. Barry Levy, "'Tender Plants': Quaker Farmers and Children in the Delaware Valley, 1681-1735," *Journal of Family History* 3 (Summer 1978): 117.
4. James A. Henretta, "Families and Farms: Mentality in Pre-Industrial America," *William and Mary Quarterly* 35 (Jan. 1978): 20-21.
5. Barry Alan Shain, *The Myth of American Individualism* (Princeton, NJ: Princeton University Press, 1994).
6. For elaborations of these arguments, see: Allan Carlson, *The Family in America: Searching for Social Harmony in the Industrial Age* (New Brunswick, NJ: Transaction Publishers, 2004): chapter 1.
7. John C. Caldwell and Thomas Schindlmeyer, "Explanations of the Fertility Crisis in Modern Societies: A Search for Commonalities," *Population Studies* 57 (2003): 241-63.

8.   Phillip Longman, *The Empty Cradle: How Falling Birthrates Threaten World Prosperity [And What to Do About It]* (New York: Basic Books, 2004).

9.   *Two Basic Social Encyclicals* (Washington, DC: The Catholic University of American Press, 1943): 5-11, 15, 55-59, 133-35.

10. See: Hubert Curtis Callahan, S.J., *The Family Allowance Procedure: An Analysis of the Family Allowance Procedure in Selected Countries* (Washington, DC: The Catholic University of America Press, 1947): 3, 68.

11. Quoted in Molly Ladd-Taylor, *Mother-Work: Women, Child Welfare, and the State, 1890-1930* (Urbana: University of Illinois Press, 1994): 91. Emphasis added.

12. On the arguably "pro-family" nature of the New Deal, see: Allan Carlson, *The 'American Way': Family and Community in the Shaping of the American Identity* (Wilmington, DE: ISI Books, 2003): 55-78.

13. Evidence for the direct positive effects of these innovations on family formation can be found in: Harvey S. Rosen, "Owner Occupied Housing and the Federal Income Tax: Estimates and Simulations," *Journal of Urban Economics* 6 (1979): 263-64; D. Laidler, "Income Tax Incentives for Owner-Occupied Housing," in A.C. Harberger and M.J. Bailey, eds., *The Taxation of Income from Capital* (Washington, DC: The Brookings Institution, 1969): 50-64; Leslie Whittington, "Taxes and the Family: The Impact of the Tax Exemption for Dependents on Marital Fertility," *Demography* 29 (May 1992): 220-22; and L.A. Whittington, J. Alms, and H.E. Peters, "Fertility and the Personal Exemption: Implicit Pronatalist Policy in the United States," *American Economic Review* 80 (June 1990): 545-56.

14. Eugene Steuerle, "The Tax Treatment of Households of Different Size," in Rudolf Penner, ed., *Taxing the Family* (Washington, DC: American Enterprise Institute, 1983): 74.

15. The full text of this report can be found in: Lee Rainwater and William L. Yancy, eds., *The Moynihan Report and the Politics of Controversy* (Cambridge, MA: MIT Press, 1967).

Appendix:
"A Primer on the 'Gay Marriage' Debate"

Featuring Eric Zorn and Allan Carlson

In October 2000, *Chicago Tribune* columnist Eric Zorn invited me to debate the issue of "Gay Marriage." This debate began in the pages of the Tribune and then continued into 2001 with further exchanges on Mr. Zorn's website, The Rhubarb Patch (see http://ericzorn.com/rhubarb/).

The initial exchange is: Copyright © 2000, Chicago Tribune Company. All rights reserved. Used with permission.

To Allan Carlson: When people of the same sex fall in love and wish to form a permanent, legal bond that at least mimics the marriage commitment, why not let them?

I'm among those who argue that the law has no business standing in the way of such arrangements, while others contend that they would harm society and so should not receive legal recognition.

The dispute has arisen in the presidential and vice-presidential debates, and to explore it in depth I've invited historian and author Allan Carlson, president of the Rockford-based Howard Center for Family, Religion and Society, to join me in the Rhubarb Patch.

He begins with a response to my challenge: "Why shouldn't the state bless gay marriages or civil unions?"

To Eric Zorn: Your question is best answered, I believe, if we first turn it upside down: Why has every healthy human society, through thousands of examples and years, restricted the special status of marriage to heterosexual pairs?

The obvious answer is that human life is naturally heterosexual: A man and a woman must come together (even if via a Petri dish) to beget new life. Reproduction is an essential task for any society, and the honor and benefits bestowed through matrimony exist to encourage and protect the act of responsible reproduction.

Centuries of folk wisdom and thousands of contemporary research inquiries in psychology and sociology also testify to a common truth: Children do best in all aspects of life if they grow and develop in an intact home with their two natural parents.

The necessary, complementary roles of fathers and mothers in child rearing enjoy their complete expression in such homes. In this setting, children will—on average—be healthier, happier, more intelligent and better adjusted than when living in any other configuration. The institution of marriage exists, then, to maximize the number of children who reside within a stable, heterosexual setting.

To extend the same honor and special benefits to gay and lesbian couples (or, by logical extension, to bisexual arrangements and "polyamorous" households) undoes, by definition, the very point of granting special status. If all group living arrangements enjoy equal "honor" and "special benefits," then no arrangement has recognizable honor or special status.   And in this case, the only proven, effective incubator of new and healthy human life would be cast aside as merely another lifestyle choice.

To Allan Carlson: You misread your history (and your Bible) if you think every healthy society has been based upon pairing off. Indeed anthropologists tell us that more than three-quarters of the cultures in the historical record, including many of those wife-intensive Old Testament nations, have allowed it.

And you misread human nature if you genuinely fear that such a modest reform as extending the legal benefits of marriage to gay couples would noticeably depress rates of "responsible" heterosexual reproduction by diminishing the status or importance of conventional marriage. Straight folks like you and me are going to keep marryin' and breedin' no matter what anyone's doing in New Town or who else is granted the "honor and special benefits" we now enjoy and that, to your mind, encourage us.

Your "on average…" argument could be—and has been!—used for all manner of social and biological engineering, just as your argument based upon nature's purpose was favored by those who opposed letting blacks and whites intermarry. But I'm sure you'd agree that even if studies showed that children of low-income, divorced or mixed race parents were "on average" likely to be less well off, it would not be an argument to forbid the poor from marrying, outlaw divorce, and reinstitute anti-miscegenation laws.

For more than 100 years this country has gradually extended rights, privileges, and respect to more and more groups. To block a further extension you have to do better than cite tradition and the wounded feelings of those who already enjoy such status.

My challenge to you as we move our exchange to the Internet is to get more specific and less theoretical: What actual harm trumps the imperative of equality and fairness to which this nation aspires?

To Eric Zorn: The issue here is not the relative degree of tolerance accorded homosexuality in past and present cultures. The issue is "same sex marriage." Outside of a few recent experiments found in Scandinavia, there are no examples in all human history of equal treatment accorded to hetero- and homosexual marriages.

Claims to the contrary, sometimes found in the gay journals, dissolve under serious scrutiny. Rather, as all the great anthropology surveys show, heterosexual marriage can be found "in every known human society," as George Murdoch writes in his book *Social Structure*. "Gay marriage" is a novelty peculiar to a few cold places during the last ten years.

You claim that, "straight folks like you and me are going to keep on marryin' and breedin' no matter what anyone's doing in New Town." But this may not be so. For nearly forty years, Americans have engaged in a broad retreat from marriage and marital childbearing. The marriage rate has fallen from 148 (per 1,000 unmarried women, ages 15-44) in 1960 to 82 in 1996, a decline of 45 percent. The re-marriage rate has fallen even faster. The divorce rate doubled over the same period, while the number of cohabiting heterosexual couples climbed from about 250,000 to 4,240,000 in 1998.

Meanwhile, births within marriage have also fallen from 4.03 million in 1960 to 2.6 million in 1997, an absolute decline of 36 percent. If one looks to the marital birth rate, the decline is 45 percent, and still continuing, toward levels portending depopulation.

Overall, the number of "nonfamily households" (dwellings without marriage or children) has soared from 7.9 million in 1960 to an estimated 31.5 million in 2000. In short, all is not well with heterosexual marriage and fertility; "marryin' and breedin'" may be disappearing.

True, the causes include basic shifts in the culture (e.g., the disappearance of favorable portrayals of marriage in the media), the economy (e.g., the decline in real male wages and the closely related flow of mothers and potential mothers into the paid labor force), and public policy (e.g., the "no fault" divorce revolution and creation of the "marriage penalty" in the federal income tax during the 1960s). Fueling such changes, though, has been the sexual revolution, which broke out of the back alleys in the 1960s and became politicized, seeking to sever the moral bonds of marriage to sexuality and child bearing, and so devalue marriage as an institution.

And this relates to your claim that this is an issue of "equal rights." It is not. Yes, it is true that some states once had laws prohibiting marriage between men and women of different races. This was wrong. But today, all Americans of certain age—even advocates for "same sex marriage"—have a Constitutionally guaranteed right to marry so long as their marriage partner is someone of the other sex. What advocates for same-sex marriage actually want is a new right, one that would allow them to change the very nature of the institution they claim to respect, and by that change further weaken it.

In one sense, then, the debate over "same-sex marriage" can be welcomed, for it forces us to confront a core question: what is marriage for?

My answer is simple: it exists because only heterosexual intimacy can produce new human life through natural births and because the accumulated wisdom of the species, as well as of all the modern sciences, tell us that stable, heterosexual, two-natural-parent homes are the superior places to rear children.

Now I grant that "social science" bears no absolute truth and that it should always be applied with care to matters of public policy. But consider your implicit argument here. You have already rejected the folk wisdom of the ages (that is, that marriage as a social institution is always reserved to heterosexual pairs). And you would, I suspect, reject the common traditional teaching of the Jewish, Christian, and Islamic faiths that homosexuality is a sin.

If you throw out social science as well (what you call the "on average..." argument), what have you left? Only ideology; only social engineering, where you summon the coercive power of the state to begin a new experiment in social relations, one necessarily involving the indoctrination of children into the tenets of sexual radicalism.

And where would you stop with your extension of this new, ideologically charged right? Should incestuous bonds (father-daughter, mother-son, or brother-sister) be blessed by society and the state? What about polygyny (one man, many wives) or polyandry (one woman, multiple husbands)? Do children have sexual rights, including the right to marry adults of their choosing?

What about "polyamorous" groups? Should "bisexuals" have the right to both a husband and a wife? And if you draw a line somewhere else, on what grounds do you deny what you call the gradual, ineluctable extension of "civil rights, legal privileges, and the benefits of our tolerance" to such unfavored groups?

But isn't homosexuality hereditary, you might retort? Alas, the frantic quest for the elusive "gay gene" remains fruitless. But even if it could be found, this would still not justify publicly sanctioned "gay marriage." It would be a powerful and morally compelling argument against other kinds of discrimination, in housing, say, or employment. But marriage exists to promote responsible procreation and superior child rearing. By definition, gay sex is always sterile, and so disqualified.

But won't science soon allow gays to clone themselves, you might persist? Anything is possible, I suppose. Yet at this point, the argument for gay marriage passes into the realm of science fiction. For me, I'll stick with other measures of truth. For in this case, the whole of human history, the teachings of the great Western religions, the common sense of the people, and the social and biological sciences all agree: marriage exists to produce and protect children; and, by nature, it can only be heterosexual.

To Allan Carlson: I don't know where you get the idea that allowing gays and lesbians to marry or form civil unions would be "coercive." In fact, to me, one of the striking features of the theoretical extension of this right to marry is how little such reforms would ask of others.

The proposal does not ask you to give up your rights nor does it threaten you or your family in any way other than the most tangential and attenuated (and, I should add, dubious) fashion that you suggest.

Your idea, if I may paraphrase, seems to be that allowing gays to form legal, socially recognized unions will indoctrinate children into the "tenets of sexual radicalism," thus harming their ability or desire to form stable, loving, heterosexual marital relationships. This in turn will lead to an increase in the percentage of children being reared in non-traditional homes and put us at risk for depopulation.

Your trend statistics are interesting, but, as you honestly observe, there have been quite a few "basic shifts in the culture" since 1960, and the cause-and-effect relationships here are exceedingly murky. We are in agreement that a host of significant legal and technological and social developments have gone into reshaping our society and changing many attitudes.

But my suspicion is that the increased tolerance of homosexuality is a very minor part of the overall equation, and my contention is that, since a small percentage of the population is always going to be gay, it's a good thing—gays have, on average, better lives than they did forty years ago.

Do you long for the days when they were even more marginalized and ostracized than they are now? Do you wish them back in the closet?

What's marriage for? Good question. Historically and currently it serves a variety of functions not limited to responsible, "superior" child rearing. If it were only about child rearing, society would discourage sterile men and women from marrying and not sanction new marriages for those women who are beyond child-bearing years.

Long-term child-free marriages would be afforded none of the rights and privileges of marriage. And once the children of a marriage were grown, the marriages would be devalued or legally dissolved.

But marriage is about more than reproduction. It's also about companionship. It's about the socially stabilizing value of sexual monogamy. It's about the power of long-term, committed partnerships to achieve more in a variety of areas than individuals can on their own.

I'm sure your marriage is about much more than just the children you and your wife have together and that many of your considerable achievements would not have been possible without the comprehensive forms of support she has provided for you over the years.

Certainly this is true in my household, and even though I suspect I got the better end of the deal my wife and I made 15 years ago when we were married, I like to think it's been a two-way-street, that our union has made both of us stronger in a variety of ways, some of which make society as a whole that much better.

I would no more deny gay people the right or opportunity to form such a union than I would deny an elderly or sterile heterosexual couple that right. They, too, can benefit from the solemnity and social recognition of permanent commitment. They, too, can find comfort and health in sanctioned monogamy. They, too, can use the solidity of a formalized, permanent relationship to do more and be more as individuals—to strengthen their communities, their workplaces, their social networks.

Marriage also has a political and property-rights dimension and is often rooted in the pragmatic needs of a society. That's why polygamy and in some cases polyandry have been sanctioned and practiced in, as I noted, the majority of societies in the archeological record.

I don't mean to write a brief for that cause—it's a bit tangential—but at the same time I could certainly imagine a Mormon version of Allan Carlson making a perfectly plausible argument that polygamy is an excellent, even superior way to raise children.

The counter-argument might be that, given our demographics, the increased numbers of men without any mates or marital prospects whatsoever would cause an overall destabilizing effect on society.

Should children be allowed to marry adults or other children? No, for the same reason that we deny other rights to children.

Should family members be allowed to marry? The biological risks of in-breeding suggest not, though I don't think that the instinctive revulsion we all feel at the idea of, say, a fifty-year-old man marrying his forty-eight-year-old sister or an adopted brother marrying an adopted sister when they have different biological parents is an intellectually honest argument against it.

Bisexual marital groupings of three or more? My view would be that, as long as the legal rights and responsibilities of all parties are clearly spelled out and understood, society would have an interest in blocking such a contractual arrangement only if significant harm could be demonstrated. What would it possibly matter if Bob and Carol and Ted down the block share a house and a really big bed and have a comprehensive contractual arrangement that obligates them to one another?

Is homosexual activity sinful? Let me stipulate that it is only in order to argue that society's right to regulate sins that occur behind closed doors between consenting adults is or at least ought to be quite limited. Lots of things are described as sinful in the great western religions that most of us here in America feel the government has no business meddling in. Sabbath breaking, for instance. Making graven images. Cursing God.

Gradually, it seems to me, we are coming around to the idea that to proscribe a certain activity, the law has to demonstrate more than just that a lot of people—the majority even—don't like it or find it distasteful.

To wit: We can't, or shouldn't, simply outlaw a drug because people like to take it because it makes them feel good. We have to, or ought to, demonstrate that the social cost of allowing the legal use of that drug creates a significant enough harm to justify making it illegal.

And this is where I think your argument so far is failing. You haven't demonstrated such harm. Speculation is simply a cousin to hysteria. Tradition is clearly related to historical abominations. Contemporary understanding of social justice demands an answer, so let me rephrase the question:

If we remove the word "marriage" from the debate, do you have an objection to gay couples being allowed to form a contractual relationship that specifies all the mutual rights and responsibilities of heterosexual marriage? And if not, which of those rights and responsibilities would you not allow them to share? Why?

To Eric Zorn: By all means, homosexuals—just as all other Americans—have the clear right to craft legal contracts allowing them to share their incomes and accumulated wealth, jointly purchase a house, promise to care for each other in sickness and old age, celebrate the holidays together, be faithful to one another, pass on all worldly goods to the survivor, and punish the party who breaks the contract. Indeed, such contracts could easily be made stronger than existing state-blessed heterosexual marriages.

"No-fault" divorce laws currently allow one partner to end—unilaterally, at will, and without penalty—a marriage, leaving the legal status of American marriage today weaker than the average business deal. By relying on private contracts, rather than frail state-blessed marriage law, gay couples would give up only a handful of public benefits (e.g., a non-working spouse's ability to claim some Social Security) and would for the reasons cited above probably be better off in the bargain.

But this route, already available, seems to have little appeal to those in the homosexual community. I suspect this is because their real goal is not to secure the material benefits of marriage. Instead, they seek public blessing for their choices and behavior, and choose to appropriate the institution of marriage to secure that imprimatur.

This I do oppose. For as I explained before, the institution of marriage—even the frail and legally battered version now found in the United States—exists to bless, protect, and encourage heterosexual bonds that will produce new human life and rear such children under optimal conditions (that is, with a father and a mother).

The fuss that we make about each new marriage—both at the wedding and in law—exists because it is only in new heterosexual unions that community renewal occurs, through the birth of children in responsibly constructed homes. Gay couples, by definition, cannot create new life. For this reason, they are denied marriage: again, by definition.

But you properly ask about those heterosexual couples who also cannot produce new life. Why should they be granted the blessing of marriage? At the level of theory, I grant that a community has less interest when two 70-year-olds marry than when two 25-year-olds do. And I think everyone instinctively understands this. Marriages among the elderly rarely draw the brouhaha, the crowds, and the nervous hopes that marriages among the young do.

All the same, sterility is not an absolute condition among heterosexual pairs. I have known many married couples who have been told by eminent medical authorities that they could not bear children and who, sometime later, were the happy parents of an unexpected baby. Would you want to institute state-run fertility tests before issuing a marriage license? For me, I am happy to respect the natural form (one man married to one woman), and let nature take its course.

Moreover, even the truly sterile heterosexual couple can still fulfill the other half of my rationale for exclusively heterosexual marriage: children grow up best in a home with both a mother and a father. This is, I repeat, a common lesson of both the social sciences and the inherited wisdom of the species. The complementarity of man and woman works even in cases of adoption, or among grandparents rearing their grandchildren. It is not just a matter of two people. One man and one woman are emotionally best equipped to rear successfully those children committed to their care. For this reason alone, even the sterile heterosexual couple deserves the state's blessing of marriage.

At another level, I suspect that our real quarrel is over the very possibility of a moral order, supported by law and public policy. You say you are ready to let the state endorse at least some incestuous marriages, "bisexual" marriages of three or more, and polygamy, in addition to gay unions. You do reject the marriage of a child to an adult of the former's choosing, but for very ambiguous reasons. I see nothing in your argument (except historical precedent which you relentlessly mock elsewhere) that would deny, say, the child of twelve his or her "sexual rights."

For me, good law openly rests on the natural order, or the natural law. On the question of marriage, revelation, common sense, and the physical and social sciences all agree: the human family order is heterosexual; our society rests on the building by men and women of the permanent sexual and economic bonds that we call marriage. And this public honor is granted because only heterosexual bonds can create new life and offer the best environment for the rearing of children.

To Allan Carlson: I think you have, in fact, exposed an element of the homosexual agenda: They want "public blessing for their choices and behavior." How outrageous of them to have the same fundamental desire for respect and recognition as moral people such as you and your wife! When they can't even procreate naturally!

You don't seem to want to deny them much in the way of fundamental contract rights ... or do you? You mention Social Security benefits as one area where no civil contract could extend those benefits conferred by the traditional marriage contract.

What about hospital visitation, probate, and so on? Specifically, which parts of the strictly legal contract of marriage do you feel should be denied to gay couples if they wanted to go about the whole thing piecemeal, making contracts with one another to cover the basket of benefits?

If the number and quality of such benefits is small to non-existent or simply insignificant, then I presume you'd have no objection to the creation of omnibus contracts, and if so, I must assume that what's inspiring your opposition here is nomenclature.

You don't want the word "marriage" co-opted by these couple who are unable to have children and whose reproductive parts don't fit together as nature intended. You don't want your government or your society to "bless" them. It strikes me, though, that it is a church or a community that "blesses" a marriage; that blessing is a religious notion and should stand apart from the law, even as marriage itself is a sacrament. Your objection to gay marriage strikes me as analogous to the objection a rabbi might make to the idea of a gentile bar mitzvah.

"Bar mitzvah" has a certain meaning among Jews and in the culture, and it would chip away at that meaning and significance if they allowed any teenaged boy of any faith who sought a solemn, sacred rite of passage into adulthood to have a bar mitzvah ceremony in their temples. I would endorse and defend that objection, so long as the state were not the provider of bar mitzvah certification. Which clearly it's not. But if it were—if the state licensed bar mitzvahs and first communions and baptisms—I would see a very knotty First Amendment problem and would be among the first to suggest that the state not be in the business of blessing various spiritual transitions and passages, and should leave those matters to the churches.

So we have two ideas, the domestic contract and the man-woman union as sanctified and blessed by a church or community. They are interwoven in the legal notion of "marriage" for, I'm sure, sound historical reasons in nations that, I'm also sure, had little or no tradition of keeping such church/state matters separate.

So if the words "marriage" and "blessing" are the sticking points, perhaps they should be relegated to the religious domain whence they came and where they belong.

Yet if I read you right, you find even the term "civil union" objectionable when it comes to gay people. This, again if I read you right, is objectionable because it suggests the state's imprimatur on their sexual conduct, which is, to put a neutral spin on it, nonproductive.

I mean, I know you like to throw around words like "immoral" and cite "natural law" when it's convenient (though I can't help observing that nature tells men to copulate with girls as young as 13 or 14, to copulate with as many females as possible, and to discard them once they have raised his young and can produce no more offspring) but let me push this issue a little further: What is it you find immoral or wrong about homosexual conduct, specifically? Is it that it is sex purely for pleasure? Is it that it employs body parts in fashions that nature did not intend or that have no conceivable natural purpose? Is it your position, then or in any case, that the law should discourage or forbid sex for pleasure or sex that employs body parts in unnatural ways?

When states have repealed their sodomy laws that applied in many cases to men as well as women, was that a mistake in your opinion? Did it send the wrong message? Should the law discourage and forbid, say, oral sex between consenting (even married) men and women? Or should we, as I advocate, mind our business when it comes to consenting adult behavior behind closed doors?

Now, about the children. The latest figures I've been able to find (feel free to update them) show than twenty-two states allow lesbians and gay men to adopt children either through state-run or private adoption agencies

After reviewing available research, the American Psychological Association concluded that "not a single study has found children of gay or lesbian parents to be disadvantaged in any significant respect relative to children of heterosexual parents," and that "home environments provided by gay and lesbian parents are as likely as those provided by heterosexual parents to support and enable children's psychosocial growth." The Child Welfare League of America and the North American Council on Adoptable Children have concluded that gays and lesbians should be treated equally in adoption application review.

"Children of lesbian mothers develop patterns of gender-role behavior that are much like those of other children," says the APA. "No data are available as yet in this area for children of gay fathers ... The data do not suggest elevated rates of homosexuality among the offspring of lesbian or gay parents. Research has shown that concerns about difficulties in personal development in these areas (separation-individuation, personality, self-concept, control, moral judgment, and intelligence) among children of lesbian mothers are unwarranted."

The contrary response to this that I could find—and, again, I trust you will do better—was griping about the inadequacy of the studies and celebrations of the nuclear family, not citation of studies that showed that the above was in error.

Is a child better off being raised in a home with a mother and a father who don't get along or where one of them is seldom present, or in a stable, loving two-mommy or two-daddy household? And at what level of optimality or sub-optimality are you willing to say the state, which you conservatives so seldom trust in other matters, should play social engineer and attempt to tell people how to live their lives and how to raise children?

One last galling point. David Miller, cited as the national field director for the Mississippi-based American Family Association, was paraphrased in an article I found on the web as objecting to gay parenting, because "homosexual relationships are less stable, and therefore children raised by homosexuals are less likely to have the 'emotional stability' to maintain social relationships."

Well, gee. Catch 22: If these relationships are, in fact, less stable than heterosexual relationships, maybe the way to making them more stable is to let them formalize their relationship in the eyes of the state. Y'think?

To Eric Zorn: Regarding benefits, I will clarify my point: homosexual pairs have the full legal right to craft private and legally enforceable contracts covering whatever law and custom might allow, including hospital visitation rights and inheritance. And there are no obstacles that I see to the development of standard contracts of this sort.

I understand there are even a few avant garde religious groups that will "bless" such unions, which should satisfy your own skittishness regarding state interference. I do not seek to deny any citizen, homosexual or otherwise, any of these opportunities. But I do oppose your attempt to take the word "marriage," as it exists in culture and law, and twist it into something radically different.

Of course, the real issue is more than that of semantics. Marriage is also an institution, the foundation of social order and community renewal, universal to the human experience. It bears these qualities because it is the responsible source of new life; it channels the powerful sexual impulse toward the creation and effective rearing of children. Marriage exists as a unique cluster of religious, social, and legal rights and obligations because of this procreative potential.

You point to the old laws forbidding or discouraging even certain forms of heterosexual contact and ask if I want them back. This is not on my agenda, for I would not want to give the modern state this intrusive power; it has too many already. But I will acknowledge that these old laws against sodomy and other practices did have one virtue: they took sexuality seriously. Without denying that pleasure was an aspect of the sexual act, these statutes implicitly underscored that more important matters were at stake.

The so-called Sexual Revolution, which broke out of America's back alleys in the 1960s, has a radically different agenda: to make the pursuit of pleasure the primary, or even exclusive, purpose of sexuality. And so the Revolution has necessarily sought to devalue marriage, and its rival claims regarding sexual purpose.

I readily acknowledge that the Sexual Revolution has unsettled things, and won some cultural victories. As The Playboy Press' own "Official History of the Sex Revolution" (entitled *The Rape of the A*P*E*—*American *Puritan *Ethic*) happily concludes: "The Revolution left a lot of devastation in its path, but nothing was reduced to less recognizable rubble than the revered...Institution of Marriage."

But then, in a remarkable fit of candor, the book also describes the broader consequences of Eros unguided: "Everything got devalued.... The American flag was devalued. Marriage was devalued. Virginity. Love. God. Motherhood.... The quality of men available to lead was devalued..., our institutions and our customs were devalued; the worth of an individual was devalued." Here, Good Ol' Hef and his friends have it about right. Sex "freed" from its procreative purpose diminishes—rather than enhances—human existence.

Marriage, even in today's battered, post-Revolution, legal form, still exists to remind men and women that sexuality has life-giving and community-renewing ends transcending that of mere pleasure. By nature—or if you prefer "by definition" (I know you dislike use of the word, "nature")—gay sexual acts cannot be procreative. They must focus on the pursuit of pleasure. Conferring the word "marriage" on such bonds denies its very meaning and the institution's first purpose. It is to diminish marriage in pursuit of other agendas.

But, you say, perhaps homosexuals can join in community renewal by adopting children. Up to this point in your argument, you have uniformly dismissed the social and natural sciences as irrelevant, or even dangerous. But here, you summon in the "available research" showing "no harm," including a pronouncement from the American Psychological Association, to buttress your case.

You really should have held to your anti-science stance. For as I think you already know, none of your evidence can pass the "keep a straight face" test. As one scholar explains in a recent issue of the *University of Illinois Law Review*, "most of the so-called 'scientific' literature which purports to show that homosexual behavior by parents has no detrimental impact upon children is methodologically flawed, based on distorted designs, small skewed samples, and a priori [non-scientific] analysis." Another researcher, Philip Belcastro, concludes that most of these studies "were biased towards proving homosexual parents were fit parents. [S]ome of the published works had to disregard their own results in order to conclude that homosexuals were fit parents." In short, a political agenda here seriously distorts the sciences.

I suppose you will call such critical responses "griping." I call them attempts to protect children from reckless social engineers. I am simply astonished at your readiness to subject children to social-sexual experimentation on this scale, in defiance of all human experience and without the backing of any reputable research. All the real evidence suggests that you would put the children so affected at great risk of negative outcomes.

The same real evidence shows that children do best growing up with their natural mother and natural father. As the mounting evidence on the long-term effects of divorce also indicates, even with parents who do not get along very well, children still do best if the adults stay together "for the sake of the children." So once again, the old wisdom proves to be true.

Marriage exists as a social and legal institution to encourage the formation and maintenance of such homes, for the sake of the children. Let it be.

To Allan Carlson: I apologize for the three-month lapse between your most recent argument and my (final) reply (per our agreement, you will have the last word after this response). I'd like to say at the outset that I think this exchange has been a success, even though it hasn't really gotten anywhere. Both of us have outlined our points completely and readers will come away with a good understanding of the differences between us.

I conclude that you have a distorted, crabbed view of homosexuality and homosexuals. What you write suggests that you view them through a keyhole that only allows you to see their sexual acts, which you find distasteful. When you see a gay or lesbian couple you make snap judgments and assumptions about the role of sexuality in their lives, their fitness to be parents, and their larger moral notions—you cannot and will not first see them as a couple, two human beings who love each other and share a great deal more than an interest in one another's gonads. And, accordingly, you hope to deny them access to full human rights and opportunities.

You do a lot of hand waving to cover up this fundamental, visceral prejudice.

Every time you fend off my hypotheticals about child rearing you back deeper into the dark corner of this position. Those who read this exchange will see that I've demonstrated that it's not really the capacity to reproduce biologically that to you validates straight-only marriage—you ultimately admit that when you allow that you have no objection to sterile or elderly heterosexual couples marrying.

And they will see also that it's not social science, either—you would not, I'm sure, suggest that mixed-race couples should not be permitted to marry even if social scientists were to show that the children of such unions had tougher lives than the children of same-race unions.

When we strip your position bare, it boils down to your personal moral notion that homosexuality is immoral, and we ought to do everything we can to discourage it and marginalize gay people.

Let me clarify my view of social science, which, for the record, I never "brand(ed) as irrelevant, or even dangerous," your assertion to the contrary. I merely pointed out to you, as I do again, that it is simply not enough to assert that some psychologists don't support the American Psychological Association's conclusion about children raised by gay couples.

You don't even tell us what Mr. Belcastro or anyone else has to say about the magnitude of these alleged harms and to what you or anyone else compares them to.

I say that if you are going to make the case that, as a matter of public policy, we should not allow gay couples to adopt children, then as a good social scientist you have first to create "adopt/not-adopt" standards. And you or any other social scientist or policy maker are welcome to do so.

Create a matrix and play with the variables...things that seem to be related to positive outcomes for children as you define them. All day long every day of the week social scientists work at isolating variables, and I'm sure with enough work they could isolate this one, as well as other variables such as income of parents, education of parents, employment status, criminal record, number of other siblings in the home, etc.

For the purposes of argument let's say that you could assign each variable a plus or minus score. And for the purposes of intellectual and scientific honesty, then, let's say you drew a bright line at a certain score: Minus 8, say. Every prospective adoptive couple scoring minus 8 on the Carlson Scale would not be allowed to adopt. That, to me, would be a defensible and honest application of social science to achieve a desired end.

What's dangerous, though, not to mention dishonest, is to pick one variable based on your moral outlook and say this variable should be determinative. It's arbitrary. It's un-American.

I am not and never was "anti-science." I am anti-sloppy, disingenuous, and the ill-motivated use of fragmentary scientific data.

What was good and what was bad about the so-called Sexual Revolution is a different discussion, yet I find the warmth with which you pick up the subject to be telling. A couple of things are worth pointing out, though: The cultural shift in our attitudes and practices regarding sexuality was not the result of one person, one institution, or some sinister outside force. It was the result of a huge number of interlocking social and even technological factors, and it should be noted that increased tolerance and rights for homosexuals came awfully late in this "revolution" and hardly led the way.

It was, in all, a popular revolution and, believe it or not, I believe you and I share some sentiments of dismay about how far things have gone in culture and entertainment. I find the shallow commercialization of sex and the stark sexual images and messages to which children are exposed depressing, even outrageous. It makes me wish people weren't the way they are, and it makes me despair of changing them. It seems to me that stressing sexual responsibility and commitment is a fine idea, but one not at all inconsistent with recognizing and even "blessing" in a secular way committed homosexual relationships. Such relationships are not, I submit, even a measurable part of the problems you identify.

It's a mistake and misleading oversimplification for you to attempt to place sexual acts into two categories—those that are procreative (good) and those that "focus on the pursuit of pleasure" (bad). Sex is so much more than that—for gay people, too, I'm told—and I'm confident that if you looked within your own life and your own situation you would recognize this. Sex is also often about intimacy, emotional sharing, profound connections, important non-verbal communications.

If I may be frank about this, my wife is no longer able to have children—she had a hysterectomy in 1998—and therefore one can say that our relations are "freed from their procreative purpose," as you put it. But I find it objectionable—hideously, offensively, contemptibly so—for you to suggest that our relations therefore diminish rather than enhance human existence.

I don't dislike the use of the word "nature," by the way. I simply point out that you toss it around freely until it boomerangs on you—your attitude toward "nature" is contradictory. Where it supports your argument, you embrace it. Where it doesn't, you ignore and hope to override it with your moral teachings.

Before turning the floor over to you to conclude, I'm going to suggest that, in the end, I think, we agree that gay couples ought to be allowed to form comprehensive, omnibus social contracts that mimic the obligations and rights of heterosexual matrimony, and we also agree that the state ought not have laws that interfere with or forbid homosexual relationships or consensual adult homosexual activity. Am I right?

If so, then I think it's a sign that though my side and your side will probably never come close to full agreement on this issue, we have found enough common ground on which to stand peacefully while the endless debating goes on.

Thanks for being such an incredibly worthy and patient adversary. Perhaps we shall tangle again on the radio.

To Eric Zorn: Since my reply marks the end of our exchange, I will confine myself to restating my key points, free of possibly misleading characterizations.

You say that I have "a distorted, crabbed view of homosexuality," engage in "hand waving to cover up this fundamental, visceral prejudice," and fail to see a gay or lesbian couple as "two human beings who love each other and share a great deal more than an interest in one another's gonads." Actually, I have said almost nothing about the nature of homosexuality or the behavior of gays and lesbians, other than reporting that homosexual sex is, by definition, always non-procreative. Since the institution of marriage exists—first and foremost and in all times and places—to encourage responsible procreation and childrearing, I logically oppose extending its prestige and benefits to same-sex couples.

My point on "social science" is simple: intact, heterosexual marriage IS the key variable in childrearing. Thousands upon thousands of research studies in all disciplines testify to a common conclusion: children raised in homes with natural parents who are married have the best prospects for growing up healthy, well-educated, productive, and happy. The core purpose of marriage law is to guide human procreation and childrearing so that the maximum number of children are born into and reared in two-natural-parent homes. To extend legal marriage to gay and lesbian couples would confuse, even subvert that core purpose.

This focus on "the good of children" explains, as well, why marriage between men and women who cannot bear children also enjoys public affirmation. They can still take part in the rearing of children through adoption, with good prospects for success because their structure still provides both a mother and a father. Their circumstance also reinforces a social model that encourages young adults toward stable, heterosexual unions. Phrased another way: when the questions is "what is best for the young," it is proper to extend the general rule (heterosexual marriage) beyond the principle purpose (procreation).

As you note, we do share common ground. I certainly do not seek to deny homosexuals their right to craft private, comprehensive contracts "that mimic the obligations and rights [relative to each other] of heterosexual matrimony" (and "progressive" churches are at liberty to bless such unions). Nor do I advocate the enforcement of anti-sodomy laws among consenting adults (because the opportunity for governmental mischief is too great). But I do assert that the public institution of marriage should be reserved exclusively for heterosexual unions. It is on this institution and through these tasks that any community—including ours—must build its future. Accordingly, marriage should not be the object for a new round of social engineering.

In closing, I want to note that I have learned from this exchange, and I have enjoyed the opportunity to be a player in The Rhubarb Patch. I look forward to our next meeting.

Index

Abrams, Kevin, *The Pink Swastika*, 63
adoption, same-sex couples and, 6
adultery, early civilization and, 7
Age of Viagra, 18
America, marriage and the New Republic, 83-85
American Woman's Home, The, 84
American Experience
    backcountry bonds and, 80-83
    cultures of marriage and, 91-93
    Family Wars and, 90-91
    marriage and baby-booms, 87-89
    marriage and the American civilization, 85-86
    marriage and the New Republic, 83-85
    Puritan Love and, 79-80
American Family Association
    gay parenting and, 124
American Psychological Association study, children of gay parents and, 123
American Puritan Ethic, *The Rape of the A*P*E**, 90, 125
Ancient Society, evolution of marriage and, 25
Augustine, *The Good of Marriage*, 12
Australia, Gross Household Product of, 36

Baker, Josephine, 103
Beecher, Catharine, *The American Woman's Home*, 84
Belcastro, Philip, study of gay parents and, 126
Bent, homosexuality and, 63
Berry, Wendell
    "Jonquil for Mary Penn, A" 47-48
    Timbered Choir, A, 46-47
Beyond Belief: The Secret Gospel of Thomas, 17
Bill of Rights

"right of privacy" and, 18
"zones of privacy" and, 14
birth control, Federal Council of Churches and, 87
Black Book of Communism, The, 69
Boston Globe, evolutionary process of marriage, 23
Bradstreet, Anne, "A Letter to Her Husband, Absent Upon Publick Employment," 13
Brand, Adolph
    Eigene, Der, 64
    homosexuality in Nazi Germany, 65
Bridenbaugh, Carl, American backcountry and, 81
Brigham Young University, campus atmosphere and, 92
Bryan, William Jennings, 86
Buchanan, Pat, procreation argument and, 6
Buchanan, Shelley, procreation argument and, 6
Bukharin, Nikolai, eliminating marriage and, 16
Burgess, Ernest W., "mutual affection" and, 32

Caesar Augustus, "Augustan Laws" and, 7
Caldwell, John C., fertility decline and, 101
Calhoun, Arthur, substitution of parentalism and, 27
Carlson, Allan
    American Psychological Association study, 123
    children and "tenets of sexual radicalism," 116
    children of gay parents and, 123
    homosexual agenda and, 121
    "Primer on the 'Gay Marriage' Debate, A," 111-131

Carpenter, Dale, procreation argument and, 6
Chang, Gene Hsin, 71
Chesterton, G. K.
    Superstition of Divorce, The, 73
    What's Wrong with the World, 73
children
    American Psychological Association study, 123
    as first purpose of marriage and, 5-19
    children of gay parents and, 123
    Christian marriage and, 9-12
Children's Bureau, creation of, 103
China, "family responsibility system" and, 73-74
Chretien, Jean, gay marriage in Canada, 23
Chrysostom, John, reasons for institution of marriage and, 11-12
Church of Jesus Christ of Latter-day Saints, cultures of marriage and, 92
Cicero, family as seedbed of virtue, 98
Civil Rights Act of 1964, 31
Clement of Alexandria, Christian marriage and, 11
Communism, communist family and, 66-71
Communist Manifesto, The, 25
Conjugal America
    cultures of marriage and, 91-93
    Family Wars and, 90-91
    marriage and baby-booms, 87-89
    marriage and the American civilization, 85-86
    marriage and the New Republic, 83-85
Conjugal Happiness
    backcountry bonds and, 80-83
    Puritan Love and, 79-80
contraception
    1917 court ruling and, 13
    Griswald v. Connecticut, 14-15
    overview of, 14-15
Coontz, Stephanie, gay movement and, 33
Cotton, John, Puritan theologian and, 80

Da Vinci Code, The, 17
Darwin, Charles, 24, 33
Davis, Kingsley, fertility decline and, 101
de Bonald, Louis

family structure and, 44
    On Divorce, 43
de Tocqueville, Alexis, 90, 93
    Americans commitment to marriage and, 83
Dean, John, suburban homes and family interaction, 29
Defense of Marriage Act, striking down of, 23
Dependent Care Tax Credit, 108
Deuteronomy, Divine blessing and, 10
Dimorphism, 34
Divorce
    early civilization and, 7
    financial burden of divorce and, 54
    no fault divorce and divorce rates, 53
    No-fault divorce, 49, 105, 119
    rates of, 2
Dole, Bob, procreation argument and, 6
Dole, Elizabeth, procreation argument and, 6
Douglas, William O., *Griswald v. Connecticut*, 14-15
Downing, William J., Defense of Marriage Act, 23

economics
    financial cost of divorce and, 54
    losing the economic function, 26-30
    new home economics and, 36-38
Education Act of 1971, 31
Eisenstadt v. Baird
    no-fault divorce, 52
    "right of privacy" and, 15
Ellingsaeter, Anne Lise, male provider norm and, 72
Encratites, Tatian and, 9
Engels, Friedrich
    marriage as union of sexual and economics, 25-26
    Origin of the Family, Private Property and the State, The, 67
Epictetus, controlling human desires and, 10
Europe, family policy as fascist and, 59
Evolutionary Psychology, ancestors reproductive strategy and, 34

Family, The, 32
Family Wars, 90-91

Federal Council of Churches, birth control and, 87
Federal Marriage Amendment, 18
Federal Smith-Lever Act of 1917, 86
feminism, women and the welfare state, 45-46
fertility rates, statistics for, 51
Franklin, Benjamin, 81-82, 89-90
Freedom to Marry, "The Marriage Resolution," 41
French Civil Code of 1801, 42
Friedan, Betty, *The Feminine Mystique*, 30
Friedlander, Benedict
homosexual rights and, 64
"Renaissance of Uranian Erotica" and, 64
Frost, Kem Thompson, 50

Gay marriage
children of gay parents and, 123
"gay gene" and, 115
historical record and, 112
homosexual activity and, 118
homosexual agenda and, 121
Genesis, fruitful wives and, 10
Germany's National Vice, 63
Glazer, Nathan, *We Are All Multiculturalists Now*, 79
Gnostics
abuse of the Eucharist and, 8-9
challenge to early Christian movement and, 8
ideas on marriage and children, 9
new Gnostics and, 17-18
"secret knowledge" and, 8
Good of Marriage, The, 12
Goode, William J., 28-29
Goodman, Ellen, gay marriage as evolutionary, 23
Goodridge v. Department of Public Health, 5
Gordon, Linda, birth control and, 13
Gospel According to the Egyptians, 9
Gospel of Thomas, "Every woman who...," 9
Graham, Billy, 87
Griswald v. Connecticut, 14-15, 32
Gross Household Product, 36

Henretta, James, raising children and, 99

Hess, Rudolph, 65
hillbillies, 80-83
Himmler, Heinrich, 62
Hindus, Michael, sexual revolutionaries and, 84
Hitler, Adolph, 62, 65
homeschoolers, division-of-labor and, 38
homosexuality
early civilization and, 7
Nazi Party and, 63
Hooker, Thomas, Puritan theologian and, 80
Hoover, Herbert, 27
Huntford, Roland, "The New Totalitarians" and, 71-72

Igra, Samuel
Germany's National Vice, 63
Thule Society and, 65
illegitimacy, marriage and, 15-17
Immerman, Ronald, ancestors reproductive strategy and, 34
Institute for Sex Research, Nazi Party raid and, 66
Ironmonger, Duncan, home-centered activities and, 36

Jackson, Gabriel, homosexuals in Nazi Party and, 66
Jansen, Wilhelm, homosexual rights and, 64
"A Jonquil for Mary Penn," 47-48
Josephus, procreation and, 10

Keillor, Garrison, 46
Kellor, Frances, 86
Kelly, Florence, 103
Kerry, John, procreation argument and, 6
Kerry, Teresa Heinz, procreation argument and, 6
Kollontai, Alexandra, *Komunistka* and, 67
Kollontai, Alexandra, 67-68
Koonz, Claudia, 60-62
Mothers in the Fatherland: Women, the Family, and Nazi Politics, 60
Kulaks, 69-70

Lanz von Liebenfels, Jorg
"Order of the New Temple" and, 65
Ostara journal, 65

Lathrop, Julia, 103
Law of 12 Brumaire, 16
Lawrence v. Texas
    Antonin Scalia dissent, 6-7
    sexual expression and, 15
Lesbian mothers, children of, 123
Lewis, C. S.
    Mere Christianity, 97
    purposes of government and, 97
Lively, Scott, *The Pink Swastika*, 63
Locke, Henry J., "mutual affection" and,
    32
Look, "Motherhood: Who Needs It?"
    article, 32
Lovejoy, C. Owen, reproductive behavior
    of man, 33-34
Luther, Martin, 48
procreation and, 12
Lyttkens, Sonja, Swedish tax code and,
    72

marriage
    as union of the sexual and economic,
        23-38
    children as first purpose of, 5-19
    Christian marriage and, 9-12
    communal nature of, 41-55
    "Conjugal Happiness" and the Ameri-
        can experience, 79
    cultures of, 91-93
    evolution of, 2
    "Evolution of Marriage, The" and,
        24-26
    extended family and, 45-46
    faith and science, 33-36
    feminism and, 30-31
    first marriage and fertility rates, 51
    five concentric rings of community
        and, 2
    *Goodridge v. Department of Public
        Health*, 5
    hillbillies and, 80-83
    historical challenges to, 42-44
    in American history and, 3
    lasting morality and, 13-14
    legal qualities and, 1
    losing the economic function, 26-30
    marriage policy and, 3
    necessity of marriage policy and, 97-
        108
    new home economics, 36-38

No-fault divorce, 105
    on illegitimacy, 15-17
    political nature of, 3
    "Primer on the 'Gay Marriage' De-
        bate, A," 111-131
    procreation and, 2
    public meaning of, 1-2
    same-sex marriage as policy issue, 1
    sex and civilization and, 7-9
    sexual evolution and, 31-33
    society's dependency problem, 45
    Stoic ideal and, 10
    virtue and the political state, 59-75
marriage policy
    centralizing state and, 98-100
    European and American models,
        102-104
    "modernity" and social crisis, 100-
        101
    necessity of, 97-108
    new marriage policy and, 106-108
    the 1960s and beyond, 104-106
Marx, Karl, 67
McDannell, Colleen, pious marriages
    and, 84-85
Mein Kampf, 62, 65
Miller, David, gay parenting and, 124
Mills, Wilbur, "marriage bonus" and,
    18-19
Milton, John, 52-53
Modernity
    fertility decline and, 101
    social crisis and, 100-101
morality, lasting morality and, 12-14
Morgan, Edmund, *The Puritan Family*,
    79
Morgan, Lewis, *Ancient Society*, 25
"Motherhood: Who Needs It?" 32
Moynihan, Daniel P., *The Negro Ameri-
    can Family: The Case For National
    Action*, 106
Murdoch, George, *Social Structure*, 113
Murdock, George, nuclear family as uni-
    versal human social grouping, 24
Murray, Jacqueline, evolution and gay
    marriage, 23
Myrdal, Alva, "Report on Equality" and,
    72
Myth of American Individualism, The,
    82

National Housing Act, FHA mortgage program, 104
Nations, nation as community, 51-55
Nazi Family System, 60-63
Nazi Party
   homosexuality and, 63-66
   Institute for Sex Research and, 66
   "Night of the Long Knives" and, 63
Negro American Family: The Case For National Action, The, 106
No fault divorce, 105, 119
   divorce rates and, 53
Noonan, John
   Christian marriage and, 11
   Gnostic forms and, 9
Novosibirsk, archives of, 70

Ogburn, William
   American birthrates and, 31
   "material culture" and, 27
Origin of the Family, Private Property, and the State, The, 25, 67

Pagel, Elaine, Beyond Belief: The Secret Gospel of Thomas, 17
Parsons, Talcott
   "auxillary" functions of family, 28
   housewife role and, 30
Pateman, Carol, feminism and, 45
Philo, Roman pleasure-seeking and, 10
Pink Swastika, The, 63
Piven, Frances, women and the welfare state, 45-46
Playboy Press
   "Official History of the Sex Revolution," 90
Rape of the A*P*E*, The, 125
Polish Sociological Review, developments in Uzbekistan and, 73
Pope Leo XIII, Rerum Novarum (The New Age), 102
Pope Pius XI, Quadragesimo Anno (Forty Years After), 102
"Population Bomb," 32
population policy, "population bomb" and, 105
Postrel, Virginia, evolutionary process of marriage, 23
Powell, Mary, 52
Powell, Richard, 52
Proceedings of the National Academy of Science, The, dimorphism and, 34

Proclamation on the Family, cultures of marriage and, 92
Puritan Family, The, 79
Puritans, 79-80

Rape of the A*P*E*, The, 125
   American Puritan Ethic and, 90
Reagan, Ronald, "The Evil Empire" and, 70
Reimer, Svend, housing attitudes and, 29
Religion
   community of faith and, 48-51
   Second Great Awakening and, 84
Rhubarb Patch, web site for, 111
Rohm, Ernst, 63
Roosevelt, Franklin, 104
Roosevelt, Theodore, 45, 85, 90
Rostow, Walt W.
   "Basic National Security Policy" report, 89
   "The American Style" and, 89
Rousseau, Jean-Jacques, "natural" marriage and, 43
Rufus, Musonius, controlling human desires and, 10

Salome, Gospel According to the Egyptians, 9
same sex marriage, as policy issue, 1
Scalia, Antonin, Lawrence v. Texas dissent, 6-7
Scholtz-Klink, Gertrude, 60-61
Schramm, David, financial burden of divorce and, 54
Science, reproductive behavior of man, 33-34
Second Great Awakening, religious participation and, 84
Seneca, adultery and, 11
Sexual Revolution, 125, 128
sexuality, sexual experimentation and, 32
Shain, Barry
   "familial inependence" and, 99
   Myth of American Individualism, The, 82
Sheppard-Towner Act of 1921, 103
Smith, Adam, 82, 90
Smith, Daniel Scott, sexual revolutionaries and, 84
Smith-Hughes Act, federal education policy and, 29
Smith-Lever Act of 1917, 86

federal education policy and, 29
Smith-Lever Vocational Training Act of 1917, 103
Social History of the American Family, 27
Southern Baptist Convention (SBC), cultures of marriage and, 91
Soviet Family Law Code, 16
Stalin, Joseph, 16, 69
statistics
    baby boom and, 87-88, 91
    births within marriage and, 114
    fertility rates and, 86
    financial cost of divorce and, 54
    first marriage and fertility rates, 51
    Gross Household Product, 36-37
    marriage boom and, 87-88, 91
    marriage rates and, 104-105, 113
    "nonfamily households" and, 114
    pregnancy and, 84
    religious participation and, 84
    size of government and Gross National Product, 99
    Utah fertility rates and, 92
Stoic ideal, 10
Stowe, Harriet Beecher, *The American Woman's Home*, 84
Superstition of Divorce, The, 73
Sweden, "Red Years" (1967-76), 16, 71-72

Tatian, Encratites and, 9
Temporary Assistance to Needy Families (TANF), 54, 107
Thule Society, 65
Toronto Globe, evolution of gay marriage, 23
Tung, Mao Tse, 74

U.S. Children's Bureau
    "Baby Saving," 86
    "Little Mothers Leagues," 86

Universal Declaration of Human Rights, 59, 106
University of Illinois Law Review, study of gay parents and, 126

Veterans Administration (VA), mortgage program and, 104

Waite v. Waite, "no fault" divorce and, 50
Washington, George, procreation argument and, 6
We Are All Multiculturalists Now, 79
We Are Everywhere, "Gay-Lesbian-Bi-Sexual" sourcebook, 64
web sites, Rhubarb Patch, 111
weddings, traditional Christian service and, 42
Wells, Robert, *Population Studies*, 83
Wen, Guanzhong James, 71
Westermarck, Edward, marriage as primeval habit, 24
Why Marriage Matters, 14
Winthrop, John, letters to his wife and, 80
Wolfson, Evan
    "gay marriage" movement and, 5-6
    Why Marriage Matters and, 14
World Congress of Families, marriage policy and, 106

Young, R. V., 49

Zorn, Eric
    legally enforceable contracts and, 124
    moral order and public policy, 120
    "No-fault" divorce and, 119
    "Primer on the 'Gay Marriage' Debate, A," 111-131
    Sexual Revolution and, 125
    "social science" and, 130
    University of Illinois Law Review and, 126